California, New Mexico, Arizona, Nevada, Colorado, Utah: these were the prizes of the bloody Mexican War. The acquisition of nearly one-third of the Mexican Empire was a turning point for the United States. Such rapid territorial growth led the North and South to quarrel bitterly over the future of these new lands—would they become slave or free? These quarrels advanced the nation down the road to disunion and civil war.

Milton Meltzer describes vividly the westward thrust of the nation under the banner of Manifest Destiny, and shows how the war was the product of these expansionist forces, carefully engineered by President Polk. Hysteria following the declaration of war produced a ready supply of enthusiastic volunteers to be pitted against raw and poorly trained Mexican conscripts.

Contemporary accounts shed new light on the decaying social and political situation within Mexico, which lessened her chances for a successful defense. Original documents clarify the intrigues and maneuvering of the war years. Meltzer has also included a special chapter on American soldiers whose dissent was so strong that they chose to desert and fight for Mexico rather than support United States policy.

Bound for the Rio Grande is a skillful portrayal of this time of intense political and ethical schism and of the complexities of a war which many considered unjust, unnecessary and plainly immoral.

The Living History Library

General Editor: John Anthony Scott

BOUND
FOR THE
RIO GRANDE
The Mexican Struggle
1845-1850

MILTON MELTZER

Illustrated with contemporary prints and photographs

ALFRED A. KNOPF : NEW YORK

THIS IS A BORZOI BOOK PUBLISHED BY ALFRED A. KNOPF, INC.

Copyright © 1974 by Milton Meltzer

All rights reserved under International and Pan-American Copyright
Conventions. Published in the United States by Alfred A. Knopf, Inc.,
New York, and simultaneously in Canada by Random House of Canada
Limited, Toronto. Distributed by Random House, Inc., New York. Maps
by Edward Malsberg. Manufactured in the United States of America.

Library of Congress Cataloging in Publication Data

Meltzer, Milton, 1915– Bound for the Rio Grande. (The Living history library)
    SUMMARY: Traces the causes, events, and aftermath of the Mexican
War, including quotes from contemporary sources and discussions of
the social and political climate of the country at the time. 1. United
States—History—War with Mexico, 1845–1848—Juvenile literature.
[1. United States—History—War with Mexico, 1845–1848] I. Title.
E404.M44 1974 973.6′2 73-15114 ISBN 0-394-82440-7 ISBN
0-394-92440-1 (lib. bdg.)

Grateful acknowledgment is made for permission to reprint copyrighted
material:

Harper & Row, Publishers, Inc., pages 40–41 of *My Confession* by
Samuel E. Chamberlain, copyright © 1956 by Time, Inc. Reprinted
by permission of Harper & Row, Publishers, Inc.

CONTENTS

BOUND
FOR THE
RIO GRANDE

1

OFF FOR THE RIO GRANDE!

At last the order to move south had come. After sitting at Corpus Christi for seven months, young William S. Henry was more than ready. He was twenty-nine now, and a restless lieutenant in the U.S. Army. In his diary he wrote:

We are off for the Rio Grande! Colonel Twiggs, with the 2d Regiment of Dragoons, and Major Samuel Ringgold, with company of Horse Artillery, left at ten this morning; officers and men were in tip-top health and spirits, and all eager to reach our extreme southwest boundary. Old "Davy Branch," the major's trusty and beautiful charger, after gaining laurels on the turf, is equally ready to reap them on the battle-field, under his gallant and accomplished owner. . . .

We reached the river at 11 o'clock. The far-famed and much-talked-about waters rolled beneath us, and the city of Matamoros rose like a fairy vision before our enraptured eyes. . . .

Two hours after our arrival a flag-staff was erected, under the superintendence of Colonel Belknap, and soon the flag of our country, a virgin one, was seen floating upon the banks of the Rio Grande, proclaiming in a silent but impressive manner that the "area of freedom" was again extended. As it was hoisted the band of the 8th Infantry played "The Star-Spangled Banner," and the field music "Yankee Doodle." There was not ceremony enough in raising it. The troops should have been paraded under arms, the banner of our country should have been hoisted with patriotic strains of music, and a national salute should have proclaimed, in tones of thunder, that "Liberty and Union, now and forever, one and inseparable," had advanced to the banks of the Rio Grande.

It was March 28, 1846. General Zachary Taylor, on the order of President James Polk, had brought Lieutenant Henry and four thousand other young men to the Rio Grande, where they stood ready to fight the Mexicans.

For what?

Best to look for the answer in the perspective of that time. A Kentuckian, for instance, said:

What do I consider the boundaries of my country, sir? Why sir, on the east we are bounded by the rising sun, on the north by the aurora borealis, on the west by the precession of the equinoxes, and on the south by the Day of Judgment.

That was the way many Americans talked about their nation's destiny in the 1840s. In that restless decade "the genuine Yankee," said a Boston newspaper, "would not be able to repose in Heaven itself if he could travel farther westward. He MUST go ahead."

And go ahead they did, by the thousands, often with

no regard for what stood in their way—rivers, mountains, deserts, wild animals—or the people who were there before them and thought they had a prior right to the land.

That part of the continent which comprised the nation was only thinly settled. In 1840 the total population of the United States was 17 million, including almost 3 million black people. Today, that number of people live in New York State alone. In 1840 about 10 million lived on the Atlantic slope, 6 million in the Mississippi Valley, and 1 million along the Gulf of Mexico. The nation was organized into 26 states and 3 territories (Florida, Iowa, and Wisconsin). The "West" in those early days was much closer. The boundary line ran northward along western Louisiana, Arkansas, Missouri, and Illinois, and then along the vast and vague edges of the Wisconsin and Iowa territories. On the other side of that line were the Republic of Texas and the Republic of Mexico, from which the Texans had recently wrested their independent nation. The Pacific slope was Mexico's California territory, all the way up to Oregon country, where Americans disputed Canadian boundaries with the British.

The United States was still an infant nation—so young, in fact, that 21,000 veterans of the American Revolution were still alive and drawing service pensions. Americans were an agricultural people. The great majority lived on farms. In the North, most farms were owned by the families that worked them, though some were rented. They raised almost all the food needed for home use, and perhaps some wheat, corn, cattle, or horses for sale. In the South, large plantations predominated. Black slaves, laboring in work gangs, raised commercial crops of cotton, sugar, rice, indigo, or tobacco.

Changes in farming could be noted at the time in New York, Pennsylvania, and Ohio. Farmers started to sell more crops and to buy more of the things they needed. The number of village handicraftsmen dwindled, while the village merchant enlarged his trade. Year by year more land went under cultivation in the region north of the Ohio and Missouri rivers. Each summer about twenty thousand new farms could be counted.

If the migrating farmer was to succeed, he had to have both transportation and a workable system of exchange and marketing. Highways were few, and it took forever for the clumsy wagons to get anywhere. Shipping was so important that it stood next to farming as a means of earning a living. The ocean marine took care of the foreign and coastal trade. New steamboats carried both merchandise and passengers along the coast and into the interior. New canal systems connected East and West, but when they proved too slow for this bustling generation, men bent their mechanical talents to perfecting the railroad that would one day replace them. Washington, the national capital, looked like a village. It had one paved road, Pennsylvania Avenue. Pedestrians and carriages moved with difficulty along streets deep in mud or dust, their way often blocked by foraging hogs or cows. Oil lamps atop wooden posts did less to penetrate the darkness than the frequent fires that broke out in the wooden or brick homes scattered on each block. Hotels were few, and most diplomats and congressmen were obliged to live in boarding houses. Except for horse races and infrequent lectures, recitals or plays, public enter-tainment was scarce.

Dueling had recently been outlawed in the District of Columbia, but violent excitement could be expected at almost any session of the Congress. There, members de-bated issues with a fierce passion that sometimes erupted into canings, whippings, or fist fights.

New York was the nation's biggest city, but its 300,000 inhabitants had not yet pushed past 23rd Street. Beyond this point were the rural areas where the wealthy built summer homes. The skyline was a palisade of ship's masts. Broadway's cobblestones clattered with horse-drawn traffic from the Battery to where the wide road thinned out to country lane four miles away. The green before the City Hall was *the* park; and the Astor House was *the* hotel, boasting three hundred rooms at a dollar a day.

In the eyes of Massachusetts writer Lydia Maria Child, who came to town to edit an abolitionist paper, New York was "this great Babylon," a scene of "magnificence and mud, finery and filth, diamonds and dirt, bullion and brass." Its contrasts struck her: "Wealth dozes on damask couches while poverty camps on the dirty pave-ment. There, amid the splendor of Broadway, sits the blind Negro beggar, with horny hand and tattered gar-ments, while opposite to him stands the stately mansion of the slave trader."

Philadelphia, with one-third fewer people than New York, was America's second city. Boston had a population of 93,000; and New Orleans, the leading city of the South, 102,000. From Buffalo, the gateway to the West, thousands took steamers for Cleveland or Detroit and then, by stage, by ship, by foot, or by horse, they pushed farther into the heart of the vast continent. From Cincinnati and Saint Louis, too, they went, leapfrogging across the country, an unending stream of humanity, each following his own dream of happiness.

To go from New York to Boston meant travel by boat, rail, and stage combined. It took six hours to get from New York to Philadelphia; almost ninety hours to reach Charleston. A journey to New Orleans lasted nearly two weeks. From New Orleans, the run up the Mississippi River to Saint Louis could be done in four days—if you were aboard one of the record-breaking steamboats and it did not blow up before you arrived.

To entertain you on such long trips there was plenty to read. Most of it was trash: *Nellie, the Ragpicker's Daughter*; *The Diary of a Hackney Coachman*; *Who Shall Be Heir?*; *The Drooping Lily*; and, remarkably like some of our modern best sellers, such titles as *The Art of Love, or How to Woo and How to Win* (translated from the French and illustrated).

Other and better books were also written—by Byron, Tennyson, Dickens, and Scott from Britain, and by the American poets Longfellow, Lowell, Whittier, Holmes, Bryant. Emerson had begun writing his essays, Cooper his novels, Melville his South Sea romances, Hawthorne his sketches.

Most readers, however, turned to the newspapers first. A revolution was taking place in journalism. The big and stodgy four-page sheets that had bored readers since Ben Franklin's time with their interminable sermons and speeches were giving way to the penny press. Newsboys raced all over the city, hawking daily papers priced at one cent—a price everybody could afford. And for the first time there was real news, fresh news, news gathered by that rising professional, the reporter. The *New York Sun* went its rivals one better, offering scandals, miracles, and horrors. The *New York Herald* invented the personal interview and concentrated on the sensational. In April 1841 young Vermonter Horace Greeley entered the field with his *New York Tribune*, another penny paper—but with a difference. Greeley would use the modern methods of journalism "to advance the interests of the People, and to promote their Moral, Social and Political well-being." Such papers influenced the whole country, giving America the news, albeit news selected and distorted by the newspaper owners' peculiar prejudices and politics.

It was a singing age, too. Ballads poured from the presses to be tried on the pianos that decorated every respectable parlor. Stephen Foster was writing enormously popular melodies, spreading his version of black life in the South. Some composers looked to other sources for inspiration. One of the favorites of the 1840s was *The Indian's Complaint*:

Oh, why does the white man follow my path
Like the hound on the tiger's track?
Does the flush on my dark cheek waken his wrath,
Does he covet the bow on my back?
He has rivers and seas where the billows and breeze
Bear riches for him alone;
And the sons of the wood never plunge in the flood

Which the white man calls his own . . .
Then go back from the red man's track,
For the hunter's eyes grow dim,
To find that the white man wrongs the one
Who never did harm to him . . .

Some did more than sing sad songs about the oppressed. Responding to the ideals that had inspired the
Declaration of Independence, they tried to right wrongs.
Theirs was an optimistic faith in man's power to make
the new nation fulfill its promises. Americans had
founded a democracy, but much more was needed to
perfect it. And nothing less than perfection would do.
What is man born for, Emerson asked, "but to be a
Reformer, a Remaker of what man has made, a re-
nouncer of lies, a restorer of truth and good?"

A tide of reform flooded the country in the early
1840s. Boston, at the heart of it, saw a convention assemble at the Chardon Street Chapel. They came from
many places and called themselves the Friends of Universal Reform. Emerson described them:

Men of every shade of opinion from the straitest
othodoxy to the wildest heresy, and many persons whose
church was a church of one member only. A great variety
of dialect and of costume was noticed; a great deal of
confusion, eccentricity, and freak appeared, as well as of
zeal and enthusiasm. If the assembly was disorderly, it
was picturesque. Madmen, madwomen, men with
beards, Dunkers, Muggletonians, Come-Outers, Groan-
ers, Agrarians, Seventh-day-Baptists, Quakers, Abolitionists, Calvinists, Unitarians and Philosophers—all came

successively to the top, and seized their moment, if not their hour, wherein to chide, or pray, or preach, or protest.

Such men and women, singly or as part of newly formed organizations, took up the battle against privilege and injustice. They attacked the new factory system for employing women and children for cruelly long shifts at pitiful wages, the landlords for the slums spreading in the cities, the southern planters for the sin of slavery, governments for seeking to settle their differences by war, men for treating women like chattels. They took up the causes of prison reform and of decent treatment for the handicapped and the insane. They fought for free schools, for equality of taxation, for labor's right to organize— and for cheap land.

2

WHAT A COUNTRY THIS MIGHT BE

No other nation ever expanded so far and so fast in one generation as the United States. The national frontier leaped from the banks of the Mississippi to the shores of the Pacific. The greatest growth took place in the 1840s.

Why did Americans go west? Men had many motives, but the strongest was hunger for land. "I ain't greedy for land," said one frontiersman. "All I want is jist what jines mine." So long as good land was rumored ahead, the pioneer would not stop. The great distances to be traveled, the terrible hardships to be overcome, the unfamiliar borders to be crossed—none of these things would frighten him.

Push-pull forces powered the great migrations. If unhappy where they were, and drawn by better opportunity somewhere else, people might risk a move. And the devastating Panic of 1837 made its victims think it would be easier to ride out hard times "anyplace but here." Luring them from home, too, were reports of rich lands in the Far West, lands to be had just for the taking.

Much of that land lay on the fringes of the vast Spanish-Mexican empire, in the provinces of California and

New Mexico. They were Spanish in little more than name. In California the Spanish settlers were isolated minorities raising sheep and cattle in a beautiful wilderness where Indian peoples pursued their aboriginal hunting and gathering existence. In New Mexico, from the endless vistas of the White Sands to the heights of the Sangre de Cristo, Spanish settlements were confined to green strips along the Rio Grande, the Rio Chama, and the San Luis.

The writings of travelers familiarized Yankees with the beauty and riches of California. One voyager was young Richard Henry Dana. A Boston blueblood, he had fallen ill while studying at Harvard. On his doctor's advice he signed on as ordinary seaman aboard the brig *Pilgrim*, one of a fleet of vessels owned by Bryant, Sturgis & Co., which bought hides and tallow from the owners of California's huge herds of cattle. The hides went to New England's rising shoe industry and the tallow to make the candles that lit the silver mines of Peru. The trader's agents and crews inevitably became promoters of the prosperity to be found on the Pacific slope.

The *Pilgrim* made the hazardous voyage around Cape Horn; 150 days out of Boston it reached port in California. Twenty-year-old Dana kept notes on his experiences and in 1840 published the classic *Two Years Before the Mast*. His book found a public eager to know what California was like. California was then part of the Republic of Mexico, which had recently won independence from Spain.

As Dana's brig beat its way up the coast to the bay of Monterey, he wrote:

The shores are extremely well wooded (the pine abounding upon them), and as it was now the rainy season, everything was as green as nature could make it— the grass, the leaves, and all; the birds were singing in the woods, and great numbers of wild fowl were flying over our heads. . . . The town lay directly before us, making a very pretty appearance; its houses being plastered, which gives a much better effect than those of Santa Barbara, which are of a mud-color. The red tiles, too, on the roofs, contrasted well with the white plastered sides, and with the extreme greenness of the lawn upon which the houses—a hundred in number—were dotted about, here and there, irregularly.

Dana described how the Californians looked:

The officers were dressed in the costume which we found prevailed through the country. A broad-brimmed hat, usually of a black or dark-brown color, with a gilt or figured band round the crown, and lined inside with silk; a short jacket of silk or figured calico (the European skirted body-coat is never worn); the shirt open in the neck; rich waistcoat, if any; pantaloons wide, straight, and long, usually of velvet, velveteen, or broadcloth; or else short breeches and white stockings. They wear the deerskin shoe, which is of a dark-brown color, and (being made by Indians), usually a good deal ornamented. They have no suspenders, but always wear a sash round the waist, which is generally red, and varying in quality with the means of the wearer. Add to this the never-failing cloak, and you have the dress of the Californian.

He paid special attention to the women:

The women wore gowns of various texture—silks, crape, calicoes, etc.—made after the European style, except that the sleeves were short, leaving the arm bare, and that they were loose about the waist, having no corsets. They wore shoes of kid, or satin; sashes or belts of bright colors; and almost always a necklace and earrings. . . . They wear their hair (which is almost invariably black, or a very dark brown) long in their necks, sometimes loose, and sometimes in long braids; though the married women often do it up on a high comb. Their only protection against the sun and weather is a large mantle which they put over their heads, drawing it close round their faces, when they go out of doors, which is generally only in pleasant weather. . . .

Generally speaking, each person's caste is decided by the quality of the blood, which shows itself, too plainly to be concealed, at first sight. Yet the least drop of Spanish blood, if it be only of quadroon or octoroon, is sufficient to raise them from the rank of slaves, and entitle them to a suit of clothes and to call themselves Españolos, and to hold property, if they can get any.

The New Englander did not show much respect for the Californians when he discussed business:

Our cargo was an assorted one; that is, it consisted of everything under the sun. We had spirits of all kinds (sold by the cask), teas, coffee, sugars, spices, raisins, molasses, hard-ware, crockery-ware, tin-ware, cutlery, clothing of all kinds, boots and shoes from Lynn, calicoes and cottons from Lowell, crapes, silks; also, shawls, scarfs, necklaces, jewelry, and combs for the ladies; furniture; and in fact, everything that can be imagined; from Chinese fire-works to English cart-wheels—of which we had a dozen pairs with their iron rims on.

The Californians are an idle, thriftless people, and can make nothing for themselves. The country abounds in grapes, yet they buy bad wine made in Boston and brought round by us, at an immense price, and retail it among themselves at a reál (12½ cents) by the small wine-glass. Their hides too, which they value at two dollars in money, they give for something which costs seventy-five cents in Boston; and buy shoes (as like as not, made of their own hides, which have been carried twice round Cape Horn) at three and four dollars, and "chicken-skin" boots at fifteen dollars apiece. Things sell, on an average, at an advance of nearly three hundred per cent upon the Boston prices.

Nor did Dana think much of the way the Californians were governed:

Revolutions are matters of constant occurrence in California. They are got up by men who are at the foot of the ladder and in desperate circumstances, just as a new political party is started by such men in our own country. The only object, of course, is the loaves and fishes; and instead of caucusing, paragraphing, libelling, feasting, promising, and lying, as with us, they take muskets and bayonets, and seizing upon the presidio and custom-house, divide the spoils, and declare a new dynasty. As for justice, they know no law but will and fear.

San Carlos mission, Monterey, California.

Over thirty thousand Indians lived at the mission stations, which Spain had begun to establish in 1769. The goal of the Jesuit, Dominican, and Franciscan missionaries was to convert the Indians and train them as farmers or craftsmen useful to Spain in guarding her distant frontiers. After the missions pioneered the new regions, herdsmen and farmers came up from Mexico to settle on the lands nearby. Dana had observed that the Indians were treated like slaves by the whites.

Of the poor Indians, very little care is taken. The priests, indeed, at the missions, are said to keep them very strictly, and some rules are usually made by the alcaldes to punish their misconduct; but it all amounts to but little. Indeed, to show the entire want of any sense of morality or domestic duty among them, I have frequently known an Indian to bring his wife, to whom he was lawfully married in the church, down to the beach, and carry her back again, dividing with her the money which she had got from the sailors. If any of the girls were discovered by the alcalde to be open evil-livers, they were whipped, and kept at work sweeping the square of the presidio, and carrying mud and bricks for the buildings; yet a few reáls would generally buy them off. Intemperance, too, is a common vice among the Indians.

What made the deepest impression on his readers, however, were passages such as this, drawing the energetic Yankee on to this new Eden:

Such are the people who inhabit a country embracing four or five hundred miles of sea-coast, with several good harbors; with fine forests in the north; the waters filled with fish, and the plains covered with thousands of herds of cattle; blessed with a climate, than which there can be no better in the world; free from all manner of diseases, whether epidemic or endemic; and with a soil in which corn yields from seventy to eighty fold. In the hands of an enterprising people, what a country this might be!

Two things were clear from the writings of Dana and others: California was rich, and the province was held only weakly by Mexico. The great ranches were supported on the labor of semi-enslaved Indians while their owners ruled like feudal barons, almost free of control by the Mexican government.

American trappers and hunters came out to California and settled down. Some behaved as they pleased, ignoring local custom and law. One of the Mexican ranchers, Guadalupe Vallejo, described what they did:

It is necessary, for the truth of the account, to mention the evil behavior of many Americans before, as well as after, the conquest. . . .

In those times one of the leading American squatters came to my father, Don J. J. Vallejo, and said: "There is a large piece of your land where the cattle run loose, and your vaqueros have gone to the gold mines. I will fence the field for you at my expense if you will give me half." He liked the idea, and assented, but when the tract was inclosed the American had it entered as government land in his own name, and kept all of it. In many similar cases American settlers in their dealings with the rancheros took advantage of laws which they understood, but which were new to the Spaniards, and so robbed the latter of their lands. Notes and bonds were considered unnecessary by a Spanish gentleman in a business transaction, as his words was always sufficient security.

Perhaps the most exasperating feature of the coming-in of the Americans was owing to the mines, which drew away most of the servants, so that our cattle were stolen by thousands. Men who are now prosperous farmers and merchants were guilty of shooting and selling Spanish beef "without looking at the brand," as the phrase went.

The severe depression that began in 1837 was felt first in the East. By the early 1840s, it was driving many from their homes in the Mississippi Valley. The bottom had fallen out of farm prices. Only bankruptcy lay ahead. There was no reason to stay where they were. Infected by California Fever or Oregon Fever, thousands sold their holdings and headed west.

Reports of the rich Willamette Valley of Oregon drew many to the Northwest. Oregon country, claimed jointly by the United States and England, had already been reached by fur trappers who crossed the northern Rockies in the 1820s and missionaries who settled there in the 1830s. The gathering point for many migrants was Independence, Missouri. The excitement that seized the town when a wagon train started its long journey was conveyed by the editor of the *Missouri Expositor:*

Even while we write, we see a long train of wagons coming through our busy streets; they are hailed with shouts of welcome by their fellow voyagers, and, to judge from the pleased expression on every face, it "all goes merry as a marriage bell" . . . and now comes team after team, each drawn by six or eight stout oxen, and such drivers! positively sons of Anak! not one of them less than six feet in his stockings. Whoo ha! Go it boys! We're in perfect Oregon Fever. Now comes on a stock of every description: children, niggers, horses, mules, cows, oxen; and there seems to be no end of them. From present evidences, we suppose that not less than two or three thousand people are congregating at this point previous to their start upon the broad prairie, which will be on or about the 10th of May.

Independence was at the same time the jumping-off point for traders going 900 miles across plains, deserts, and mountains to the southwest country of New Mexico. One early pioneer of this Santa Fe trail was Josiah Gregg, a Missourian. In bad health, he, like Dana, thought an outdoor life, a life of physical hardship, might be his cure. At twenty-five he joined a caravan setting out for Santa Fe, and spent the next nine years as a trader on that route. Gregg's book, *The Commerce of the Prairies*, appeared in 1844. It was based upon a journal he kept, and like Dana's book, it swiftly became a classic.

Gregg tells what supplies they stocked for the trail, and how the load was carried:

The ordinary supplies for each man's consumption during the journey are about fifty pounds of flour, as many more of bacon, ten of coffee and twenty of sugar, and a little salt. Beans, crackers, and trifles of that de-

Oregon City, Oregon in 1848.
Lithograph by Henry James Warre.

scription are comfortable appendages, but being looked upon as dispensable luxuries, are seldom to be found in any of the stores on the road. The buffalo is chiefly depended upon for fresh meat, and great is the joy of the traveler when that noble animal first appears in sight.

The wagons now most in use upon the prairies are manufactured in Pittsburg; and are usually drawn by eight mules or the same number of oxen.

What did the pioneers look like? Gregg's first caravan was made up of men of every social class, with a sprinkling of women—part of a Spanish family once banished but now returning to their homes. Gregg describes their clothing and weapons:

The wild and motley aspect of the caravan can be but imperfectly conceived without an idea of the costumes of its various members. The most fashionable prairie dress is the fustian frock of the city-bred merchant furnished with a multitude of pockets capable of accommodating a variety of extra tackling. Then there is the backwoodsman with his linsey or leather hunting-shirt—the farmer with his blue jean coat—the wagoner with his flannel-sleeve vest—besides an assortment of other costumes which go to fill up the picture.

In the article of firearms there is also an equally interesting medley. The frontier hunter sticks to his rifle, as nothing could induce him to carry what he terms in derision "the scatter-gun." The sportsman from the interior flourishes his double-barreled fowling-piece with equal confidence in its superiority. The latter is certainly the most convenient description of gun that can be carried on this journey; as a charge of buck-shot in night attacks (which are the most common) will of course be more likely to do execution than a single rifle-ball fired at random. The repeating arms have lately been brought into use upon the prairies and they are certainly very formidable weapons, particularly when used against an ignorant savage foe. A great many were furnished beside with a bountiful supply of pistols and knives of every description, so that the party made altogether a very brigand-like appearance.

About 150 miles out they reached the rendezvous of Council Grove. They had seen no houses or Indian camps from the first day. Here the main body of the caravan was organized, and politics came into play, as Gregg tells it:

The designation of Council Grove, after all, is perhaps the most appropriate that could be given to this place; for we there held a grand council, at which the respective claims of the different aspirants to office were considered, leaders selected, and a system of government agreed upon, as is the standing custom of these promiscuous caravans. One would have supposed that electioneering and party spirit would hardly have penetrated so far into the wilderness: but so it was. Even in our little community we had our office-seekers and their political adherents, as earnest and as devoted as any of the modern school of politicians in the midst of civilization. After a great deal of bickering and wordy warfare, however, all the candidates found it expedient to decline, and a gentleman by the name of Stanley, without seeking or even desiring the office, was unanimously proclaimed captain of the caravan.

needed, and a fortification against the Indians. Not to embarrass this cattle-pen, the campfires are all lighted outside of the wagons. Outside of the wagons, also, the travelers spread their beds, which consist, for the most part, of buffalo-rugs and blankets. Many content themselves with a single Mackinaw; but a pair constitutes the most regular pallet; and he that is provided with a buffalo-rug into the bargain is deemed luxuriously supplied. It is most usual to sleep out in the open air, as well to be at hand in case of attack, as indeed, for comfort; for the serene sky of the prairies affords the most agreeable and wholesome canopy.

Gregg traveled the Santa Fe trail eight times before he quit. As relations between Mexico and the United States deteriorated, the Mexicans tightened regulations and trading slowly came to an end. But while it lasted it had an important influence—for good and bad. The fact that the big covered wagons could make it across almost a thousand miles of rough country encouraged migrations in the future. But the troubles the frontiersmen encountered among the Mexicans created a stereotyped response that persists even today. The traders in a strange land made no attempt to understand a different culture. They blamed their difficulties on the "foreigners" and nursed a contempt for Mexican civilization. The cruel effect of severe poverty among the Mexican people was mistaken by the energetic Americans for laziness. It was but a small step to conclude that such a feeble people could easily be invaded and conquered.

3

TEXAS FEVER

The shock waves created by the Panic of 1837 rolled south to bankrupt many planters in the newer cotton lands of the Delta region. In flight from their creditors, the planters saw a nearby haven in the independent Republic of Texas. Its door was wide open to newcomers. A Texas Fever seized the southerners but left heads cool enough to plot ingenious escape without detection by the sheriff. J. A. Orr, traveling through Mississippi, tells how they managed it:

As a general thing on the evening before abandonment those large plantations would present no unusual appearance. The stock would be in the stables, properly attended to; the cows would be in the cowpen, the hogs would be called and fed; the sheep would be herded; the plantation Negroes would be in their proper places, and over all the hush of evening and the stillness of night would fall.

On the morning following the smoke would curl from the chimneys, from residence and quarters, the cows would be lowing in the pen, the sheep bleating in the fold, the hogs in their places; not a wagon gone, not a vehicle missing; the meat left in the smokehouse, the poultry raising the usual disturbance—and not a human being, nor horse, nor mule, nor saddle, nor bridle on the whole place. Every Negro, every horse, every mule spirited away in the darkness of the night—the Negro women and children on horses and mules, the men on foot, all, all in a double-quick march for Texas. . . .

The Texas these settlers came to had only recently been a province of Mexico, and before that, of Spain. Throughout most of the sixteenth century Spanish explorers had wandered over Central America looking for gold. When Cortez began his invasion of the land of the Mayas and Aztecs, the region was one of the most thickly populated of the New World. Intensive farming, vast irrigation systems, and the regimentation of labor under despotic governments had made large populations possible. The Aztecs and Mayas had developed the most sophisticated civilization in the Americas. Yet the Spaniards, with their small bands of soldiers, succeeded in making Mexico a colony of Spain. They achieved the conquest by brute force and enslaved those who survived.

Whites born in Spain, called *gachupines*, were the rulers of Spain's overseas empire. Whites born in Mexico, called *criollos* (Creoles), became the aristocracy. Their number soon was greater than the *gachupines*, but they were always kept to second place—in government, in jobs, in wealth. These two classes of whites managed to find common ground in the relentless effort to hold the Indians down, denying them schooling, jobs, and personal liberties. In time, the culture the Indians had inherited from their ancestors was obliterated.

By the end of the 1700s intermarriage between Creole men and Indian women had produced a rapidly growing class called *mestizos,* who began to demand a share in power. Part Indian, they were rated almost as low as the Indians themselves, and as a result, they clashed with both the *gachupines* and the Creoles.

Mexico's land was taken over by the Spaniards in a system of *encomiendas* that required the Indians living on the land to work gratis for the Spanish master. The ranches, called *haciendas,* grew to great size as the whites simply took more and more land from the Indians. At the same time, the Catholic church, allowed to function under its own laws and courts in Mexico, grew stronger and richer. Its officials owned vast country estates and city properties. So wealthy did the church become that much of Mexico's money fell under its control. The church was the country's banker, controlling the ranchers by holding their mortgages. Out of the mines came the wealth that built cathedrals and filled them with treasures. As rich as the church was in property, so it was poor in public spirit. It showed concern for government problems only when its own interests were threatened.

The Indians were ground between two stones: the church, professing to save their souls but doing little for their human welfare; and the state, out to gather riches and treating the Indians as machines to be worked for maximum profit.

Such a social system did little to expand the economy and raise the living standards of the mass of people. The farms, ranches, and mines were in the hands of a tiny minority. Agriculture never developed fully; neither did education, science, or the arts.

In 1810 revolt broke out. Led by a Catholic priest, Miguel Hidalgo y Costilla, its battle cry was "Independence and Death to the Spaniards!" The Indians and mestizos struggled to free themselves from the Spanish yoke, taking heart from the examples of the American and French revolutions. For years the revolutionary war went on, tearing Mexico apart, with wholesale slaughter and devastation common on both sides. It ended in 1821 when General Iturbide deserted the government side and brought his army over with him. The revolutionists had won; an independent Republic of Mexico was established.

But a disastrous pattern had been set. For decades to come, power shifted countless times as one general or another moved his army to this side or that. Power passed only by means of violence. It would take almost a century before the constant chaos and disorder would end. In the thirty-year period that immediately followed the revolution, Mexico suffered fifty different administrations. Meanwhile, the poor, who thought they had won in 1821, enjoyed no benefits from their revolution and never had the chance to decide life for themselves.

Old Mexico was the heart of the Spanish empire in the Americas. Now and then new colonies were set up in the north to fend off threats from foreign powers. New Mexico was the site of the first such colony, established in 1536. A hundred years later a few settlements were planted on the enormous landscapes of Texas and Arizona. Then, shortly before the American Revolution began, the Spanish started to build missions and forts in California.

Spain's hold on the province of Texas was never strong. In 1800 it amounted to the three small settlements at San Antonio, Goliad, and Nacogdoches, plus a few missions. To all the settlements on her northern frontier Mexico had only the most fragile ties. One reason was the great distance—a thousand miles and more —between them and the national capital at Mexico City. In the stormy years of the Mexican Revolution the outlying frontiersmen were too remote from the center to become involved. After the Republic of Mexico was founded, the home government underwent too many rapid and violent changes to be able to exercise any control over the four thousand Mexicans engaged in cattle ranching on the northern borders. Remote, isolated, they managed their own affairs.

Gradually Mexico opened the great prairies of Texas for immigration. In 1821 and again in 1823 land grants were made to people such as Moses and Stephen Austin who would bring in settlers. The immigration law was so generous in its offer of land that by 1830 the Texas population had increased fourfold. The great majority of the new immigrants came from the United States. Soon the Mexicans began to fret over the behavior of these "Anglos." The law left the colonists free to handle their own affairs. That inevitably meant life American-style, not Mexican. The immigrants had taken an oath of loyalty to Mexico, but it was plain they could not or would not break with their old ties. In 1827 the worried Mexicans sent a commission to Texas to study

Austin, Texas in 1840.

the situation. One member, José María Sanchez, noted his impressions in a journal:

The Americans from the north have taken possession of practically all the eastern part of Texas, in most cases without the permission of the authorities. They immigrate constantly, finding no one to prevent them, and take possession of the sitio [location] that best suits them without either asking leave or going through any formality other than that of building their homes. Thus the majority of inhabitants in the Department are North Americans, the Mexican population being reduced to only Bejar, Nacogdoches, and La Bahía del Espíritu Santo, wretched settlements that between them do not number three thousand inhabitants, and the new village of Guadalupe Victoria that has scarcely more than seventy settlers. . . . Repeated and urgent appeals have been made to the Supreme Government of the Federation regarding the imminent danger in which this interesting Department is of becoming the prize of the ambitious North Americans, but never has it taken any measures that may be called conclusive, either because it has always been involved in those fatal convulsions that have destroyed the republic, or because secret agents, deceiving the officials, have made them believe that all is but the exaggeration of weak and cowardly spirits. Thus the vigilance of the highest authorities has been dulled while our enemies from the North do not lose a single opportunity of advancing though it be but a step towards their treacherous design which is well known. . . .

Visiting the Texas settlement that would become the city of Austin, Sanchez could like neither the place nor the people who lived there. He warned his government of what would surely happen:

This village has been settled by Mr. Stephen Austin, a native of the United States of the North. It consists, at present, of forty or fifty wooden houses on the western bank of the large river known as Rio de los Brazos de Dios, but the houses are not arranged systematically so as to form streets; but on the contrary, lie in an irregular and desultory manner. Its population is nearly two hundred persons, of which only ten are Mexicans, for the balance are all Americans from the North with an occasional European. Two wretched little stores supply the inhabitants of the colony: one sells only whiskey, rum, sugar, and coffee; the other, rice, flour, lard, and cheap cloth. It may seem that these items are too few for the needs of the inhabitants, but they are not because the Americans from the North, at least the great part of those I have seen, eat only salted meat, bread made by themselves out of corn meal, coffee, and home-made cheese. To these the greater part of those who live in the village add strong liquor, for they are in general, in my opinion, lazy people of vicious character. Some of them cultivate their small farms by planting corn; but this task they usually entrust to their Negro slaves, whom they treat with considerable harshness.

Beyond the village in an immense stretch of land formed by rolling hills are scattered the families brought by Stephen Austin, which today number more than two thousand persons. The diplomatic policy of this empresario [land agent], evident in all his actions, has, as one may say, lulled the authorities into a sense of security, while he works diligently for his own ends. In my judgment, the spark that will start the conflagration that will deprive us of Texas, will start from this colony. All because the government does not take vigorous measures to prevent it. Perhaps it does not realize the value of what it is about to lose.

Two years later, General Mier y Terán placed the North Americans he encountered into two classes:

First, those who are fugitives from our neighbor republic and bear the unmistakable earmarks of thieves and criminals; these are located between Nacogdoches and the Sabine; ready to cross and recross this river as they see the necessity of separating themselves from the country in which they have just committed some crime; however, some of these have reformed and settled down to an industrious life in the new country. The other class of early settlers are poor laborers who lack the four or five thousand dollars necessary to buy a sitio of land in the north, but having the ambition to become landholders—one of the strong virtues of our neighbors— have come to Texas. Of such as this latter class is Austin's colony composed. They are for the most part industrious and honest, and appreciate this country. Most of them own at least one or two slaves.

Slavery was banned under Mexican law in 1829. The U.S. immigrants—nine out of ten of them were Southerners—did not like that. They pressured the Mexican government to repeal the laws, or at least make an exception for Texas. The general described the effect upon slave and master:

These slaves are beginning to learn the favorable intent of the Mexican law toward their unfortunate condition and are becoming restless under their yoke, and the masters, in the effort to retain them, are making that yoke even heavier; they extract their teeth, set on the dogs to tear them in pieces, the most lenient being he who but flogs his slaves until they are flayed.

The religious issue, too, concerned the colonists. Almost all were Protestants, but the Mexican government forbade public worship for any but Catholics. Still, economic prospects were of greater importance to the settlers.

In answer to queries from home sent by people thinking of emigrating, Mary A. Holley, living in Bolivia, Texas, wrote a letter in 1831 that said her experience was "like a dream or youthful vision realized." After praising her new Eden, she got down to realities:

You wish to know my opinion, if it will do for all sorts of people to emigrate to Texas. . . . On this point, I should say, industrious farmers will certainly do well, and cannot fail of success; that is to say, if abundant crops, and a ready market with high prices, will satisfy them. Substantial planters, with capital and hands, may enlarge their operations here to any extent, and with enormous profits.

He whose hopes of rising to independence in life, by honourable exertion, have been blasted by disappointment; whose ambition has been thwarted by untoward circumstances; whose spirit, though depressed, is not discouraged, who longs only for some ample field on which to lay out his strength; who does not hanker after society nor sigh for the vanished illusions of life; who has a fund of resources within himself, and a heart to trust in God and his own exertions; who is not peculiarly sensitive to petty inconveniences, but can bear privations and make sacrifices, of personal comfort— such a person will do well to settle accounts at home, and begin life anew in Texas.

By now the U.S. settlers so greatly outnumbered the Mexicans that they were able to force the government to modify its rulings on slavery. The colonists kept their slaves, but Mexico felt all the more strongly that the Anglos' loyalty was divided. Meanwhile, American interest in acquiring Texas became plainer by the day. Some newspapers openly campaigned for extending the American boundary to the Rio Grande. President John Quincy Adams tried to achieve expansion by purchase, offering $1 million for Texas. He was turned down. Later, President Andrew Jackson raised the offer to $5 million, but this too was politely declined. When Jackson's agent tried bribery and then suggested the use of force, what could Mexican officials think?

Fearful of losing Texas, they banned further immigration from the U.S. in 1830 and cut off the colonists' economic ties with their home country. Soldiers and customs officers were stationed on the American border. These moves fanned an already smoldering fire. Laws or no laws, the Americanization of Texas would go on. By

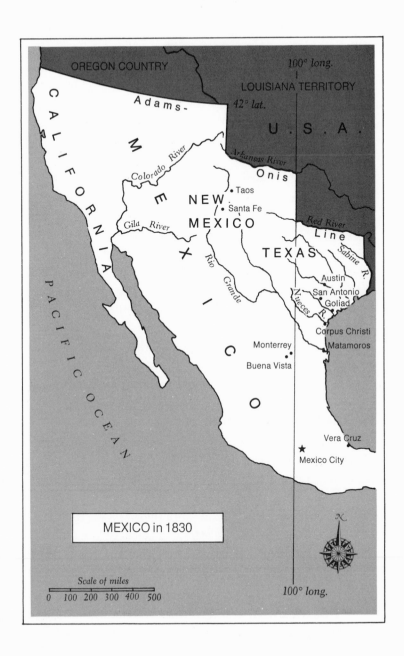

OREGON COUNTRY

LOUISIANA TERRITORY

100° long.

42° lat.

U . S . A .

CALIFORNIA

Adams-

Colorado River

Arkansas River

Onis

M

E

X

I

C

O

NEW

Taos

Santa Fe

MEXICO

Gila River

Red River

Line

Rio Grande

TEXAS

Sabine R.

Austin

San Antonio

Nueces R.

Goliad

Corpus Christi

PACIFIC OCEAN

Monterrey

Matamoros

Buena Vista

Vera Cruz

Mexico City

MEXICO in 1830

Scale of miles

0   100 200 300 400 500

100° long.

N

the end of 1835 there were 35,000 Anglo-Americans in Texas, ten times the number of Mexicans.

The gulf widened as Texans demanded the lifting of Mexican restrictions or tried to evade them. A Committee of Safety and a volunteer militia were set up to prepare for Mexican intervention. There were the usual "incidents" as the two opposing forces maneuvered. Finally the president of Mexico, General Santa Anna, put aside the Mexican Constitution in favor of a centralized system that overrode states' rights, and prepared to back his dictatorship with military power. The American settlers' reply was to form their own government, adopt a constitution modeled on the U.S. one, and place Sam Houston at the head of an army. Even at this late date, however, the great majority of the Texans voted against secession from Mexico.

To establish military control over the province, Santa Anna, with an army of 4,000, laid siege in February 1836 to a force of 187 Texans fortified in a mission building at San Antonio called the Alamo. The Mexicans lost 1,544 men before they overwhelmed the Texans. They massacred all the defenders, among them the famous fighters William Travis, Davy Crockett, and Jim Bowie.

Under the rallying cry of "Remember the Alamo!" the Texans mobilized to stop the advancing Mexican Army. At Goliad the Texans were defeated again, losing 300 men. But two months after the defeat at the Alamo, at San Jacinto, Sam Houston surprised the overconfident Santa Anna, and though outnumbered three to one, killed 600 Mexicans and captured almost all the others, including the general himself. Santa Anna signed treaties recognizing the independence of Texas, treaties that he

"The Surrender of Santa Anna," by W. H. Huddle.

and the Mexican Congress repudiated as soon as he was freed. Nevertheless, Texas went its own way from that time on, operating as the independent Lone Star Republic. Houston, elected its first president, sought annexation by the United States, a policy favored by all but a handful of the 6,000 Texan voters.

President Jackson, nearing the end of office, feared that to annex Texas would mean war with Mexico and an upheaval in domestic politics. Not until the day before he left the White House would he even recognize the Republic of Texas.

What made the annexation question so troublesome was its connection with slavery. The first laws adopted by Texas protected and regulated the institution of slavery. To many in the North that meant the annexation of Texas would add another slave state to the Union. The Texas issue could not be viewed apart from the larger struggle between those political forces that sought to preserve and extend slavery, and those that wanted to contain and overthrow it.

For several years the politicians, not yet ready to meet the slavery issue head-on, dodged any debate on annexation. Texas did not stand still meanwhile. She attracted thousands of settlers with more liberal offers of land than the United States would make. Within a decade the Texan population had jumped to 142,000. And by now, across the border, Americans were ready to act on annexation.

4

MANIFEST DESTINY

The cry for expansion was in full chorus in the 1840s, but the theme had been sounded long before. Land hunger, as we have seen, was a constant motive for expansion. It carried generations of hopeful landowners out of Europe as well as from the eastern slope of the United States into the American West. Many dreamed of tilling their own farms while others dreamed of founding new fortunes by speculating in land. And to merchants and manufacturers, the prospect of expanded borders meant new markets for their goods and services.

The imaginative were never short of ideas to justify expansion. One such idea held that symmetry in nature should be a guide to symmetry in a country's boundaries. Taking over Texas, California, and Oregon was necessary, then, to "round out" the nation's boundaries. Or there was the law of gravity to appeal to. If large bodies attracted small ones in nature, then surely large nations must attach small ones to themselves. And what about the natural law holding that all living things must grow or die? It followed that the United States must not permit its boundaries to remain unchanged. It *had* to expand them or perish.

By far the most appealing phrase to rationalize the goal of the expansionists was "manifest destiny." The man who coined it was John L. O'Sullivan, a graduate of Columbia, trained in law but working as an editor. At the age of twenty-four he had founded the *Democratic Review*, launching it on the troubled financial seas of 1837. His aim, he said, was "to strike the hitherto silent string of the democratic genius of the age and the country." From its birth the magazine advocated a national mission to spread American democracy across the North American continent. In November 1839 O'Sullivan's overblown prose was already reaching for the phrase that would put the expansionists in his debt:

The far-reaching, the boundless future will be the era of American greatness. In its magnificent domain of space and time, the nation of many nations is destined to manifest to mankind the excellence of divine principles; to establish on earth the noblest temple ever dedicated to the worship of the Most High—the Sacred and the True.

"Destined to manifest . . ." Close, but the perfect phrase would not be coined by O'Sullivan for another six years. Still, the idea was there—the vision of a great democratic power whose "floor shall be the hemisphere."

Expansion was all very well if nothing was in the way of it. But soon the American people were forced to think about war as the possible price of expansion. Texans clamored for annexation, even if it meant war with Mexico. Settlers in California talked openly of tearing that rich province away from Mexico. Up in the Willamette Valley of Oregon still other frontiersmen pushed for adding that disputed territory to the United States, no matter how it conflicted with England's rights there.

By 1844 the whole country was stirred up by the question of what to do about Texas, and also about Oregon. A national election was coming up in November. People would have a chance to speak when they chose a President.

In the White House at this time sat John Tyler of Virginia. He took up the Texas question in the hope of winning support for reelection. The British, who had recognized Texas independence in 1840, had just promised the new republic a large loan and support in securing Mexican recognition of Texas independence if Texas would consent to remain an independent republic.

Most Texans, however, still wanted to be joined to the United States. Tyler's secretary of state, John C. Calhoun of South Carolina, saw a way to fuse the expansionist fever with traditional anti-British sentiment in a drive for annexation. In April 1844, though Mexico was at peace with us, he promised to lend our army and navy to Texas in the event she went to war with Mexico. The next day he signed a treaty with Texas that called for incorporating it into the United States not as a state but as a territory. Now he had to get a two-thirds majority in the Senate to ratify the treaty.

It was not easy to do. The issue of expansion had become thoroughly entangled with the issue of slavery. Both South and North were concerned with the national balance of power. The North feared that annexation of the vast Texas territory—empowered to divide itself into five states if it so chose—would add a new slave domain and tilt the scales against the free states.

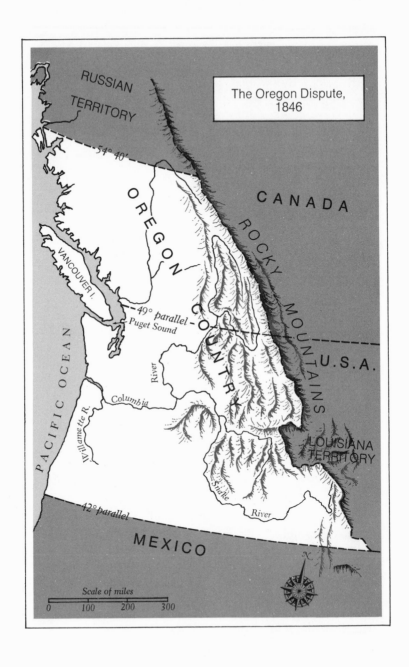

The Oregon Dispute, 1846

RUSSIAN TERRITORY

54° 40'

OREGON COUNTRY

CANADA

ROCKY MOUNTAINS

VANCOUVER I.

49° parallel
Puget Sound

PACIFIC OCEAN

River

Columbia

U.S.A.

Willamette R.

LOUISIANA TERRITORY

Snake

River

42° parallel

MEXICO

Scale of miles

0   100   200   300

Daniel Webster, the senator from Massachusetts, had years earlier voiced northern Whig feeling when he said in a speech:

Texas is likely to be a slave-holding country, and I frankly avow my entire unwillingness to do anything that shall extend the slavery of the African race on this continent or add other slave-holding states to the Union. When I say I regard slavery in itself as a great moral, social, and political evil, I only use language which has been adopted by distinguished men, themselves citizens of slave-holding states. I shall do nothing, therefore, to favor or encourage its further extension.

On the other side were such southerners as Abel P. Upshur of Virginia. "Few calamities could befall this country more than the abolition of slavery in Texas," he wrote. "We regard annexation as involving the security of the South."

Old John Quincy Adams, long an advocate of expansion, now came to see that expansion offered no guarantee of freedom over the continent. It might just as well extend the slavery he hated and had fought against for years in Congress. He published an address to the nation warning that with annexation would come the dissolution of the Union. He saw in the movement for Texas annexation a plot to create new slave states. In powerful language he built up in the public mind the frightening specter of a Slave Power Conspiracy seeking to dominate American life.

Going to the Senate with their annexation treaty, Calhoun and Tyler played what is called the "foreign devil" game. They hinted of a British plot to make

Texas her satellite and then to end slavery there, thus threatening the peculiar institution in the South. To defeat the schemers and keep Texas on the side of slavery, the nation had to annex her now, they argued.

Calhoun miscalculated. The Senate rejected his treaty by a decisive vote of 35 to 16.

Even while the Senate was debating the annexation treaty, the political parties were preparing to nominate presidential candidates. Henry Clay of Kentucky, sure of the Whig nomination, wanted to make clear his opposition to annexation. In a letter dated April 17, 1844, he wrote:

Annexation and war with Mexico are identical. Now, for one, I certainly am not willing to involve this country in a foreign war for the object of acquiring Texas. I know there are those who regard such a war with indifference and as a trifling affair, on account of the weakness of Mexico, and her inability to inflict serious injury upon this country. But I do not look upon it thus lightly. . . .

Assuming that the annexation of Texas is war with Mexico, is it competent to the treaty-making power to plunge this country into war, not only without the concurrence of, but without deigning to consult Congress, to which, by the Constitution, belongs exclusively the power of declaring war?

Then Clay, like Adams, spoke of his fear that this issue could split the country in two:

I conceive that no motive for the acquisition of foreign territory would be more unfortunate, or pregnant with more fatal consequences, than that of obtaining it for the purpose of strengthening one part against another part of the common confederacy. Such a principle, put into practical operation, would menace the existence, if it did not certainly sow the seeds of a dissolution of the Union.

Martin Van Buren, who had a majority of the Democratic delegates pledged to his candidacy, agreed with Clay that the Texas question would only divide the Union dangerously and should, therefore, not be made a party issue. So, a few days after Clay's letter appeared, he published a similar letter. But Van Buren's action stirred a revolt among Democratic party leaders. New candidates jumped into the field, denouncing Van Buren and pledging themselves to the annexation of Texas. At the convention Van Buren was defeated and the nomination given to James K. Polk of Tennessee, whose slogan was "All of Texas and All of Oregon."

At Clay's request, the Whig platform was silent on Texas annexation. The Democrats, however, trumpeted where they stood. Their national convention adopted this key resolution:

RESOLVED, That our title to the whole of the territory of Oregon is clear and unquestionable; and that no portion of the same ought to be ceded to England, or any other Power; and that the re-occupation of Oregon, and the re-annexation of Texas at the earliest practical period, are great American measures, which this convention recommends to the ardent support of the Democracy of the Union.

The spirit of Manifest Destiny, by a contemporary artist.

(Note the wording, "*re*-occupation" of Oregon and "*re*-annexation" of Texas. The Democrats implied that the United States already owned Oregon and had bought Texas from Napoleon in the Louisiana Purchase of 1803. The facts do not justify either claim.)

"Fifty-four Forty or Fight" became the campaign slogan of the Democrats. By it they demanded all of Oregon up to the 54th parallel at the tip of Alaska. It was a tactic designed to draw the sting out of the Texas issue. Since the opponents of annexation charged that the taking of Texas was a slaveholder's plot, the Democrats were cleverly coupling that plank with a demand for Britain to give up her legitimate claims to the Oregon territory. So—something for the southerners and something for the westerners.

Polk, the Democratic standard bearer, has been called the first "dark horse" candidate in American history. Van Buren had been expected to win the party nomination, but even after two successive defeats for the governorship of Tennessee, Polk took the prize.

Polk himself was not an obscure man. The Nashville lawyer had long been a leader in Tennessee politics, serving as Governor, Congressman, and Speaker of the U.S. House of Representatives. A political protégé of "Old Hickory"—Andrew Jackson—Polk had been dubbed "Young Hickory." A lean man, with gray eyes in an unsmiling face, and white hair brushed back behind his ears and down over his collar, he looked much older than he was. At forty-nine he was the youngest man until then to be elected to the Presidency.

What the inner man was like, his diary reveals. Justin H. Smith, a historian of the Mexican War, considers

Polk's diary essentially truthful, and says that combined with much other evidence it gives us this picture of Polk:

A cold, narrow, methodical, dogged, plodding, obstinate partisan, deeply convinced of his importance and responsibility, very wanting in humor, very wanting in ideality, very wanting in soulfulness, inclined to be sly, and quite incapable of seeing great things in a great way. All know the type. It is the leading citizen and schemer of the small town, who marches up the center aisle on public occasions with creaking shoes and a wooden smile, and takes his seat with a backward, all-embracing glance.

During the election campaign the partisans of expansion began to whoop it up for war. The *New Orleans Picayune* echoed the "Fifty-four Forty or Fight" challenge in its own folksy way:

Whar, I say whar is the individual who would give the first foot, the first outside shadow of a foot of the great Oregon? There ain't no such individual. Talk about treaty occupations to a country over which the great American eagle has flown! I scorn treaty occupation. Who wants a parcel of low flung, "outside barbarians," to go in cahoo with us, and share alike a piece of land that always was and always will be ours? Nobody. Some people talk as though they were affeered of England. Who's affeered. Hav'nt we licked her twice, and can't we lick her again? Lick her! yes; jist as easy as a bar can slip down a fresh peeled saplin'.

Andrew Jackson, old and feeble now, but still able to command the rhetoric politicians often use to say the

Campaign poster by Nathaniel Currier for 1844 election.

opposite of what they mean, made this appeal for voters to support the expansionist goals of his man Polk:

If there be patriotism in the effort to increase the wealth and happiness of all classes in our society—to diffuse the blessings of equal laws, and a just government—if there be love in the spirit which finds in this free land of ours the means to spread the light of the Gospel, and to teach fallen man throughout the world how he may recover his right to civil and religious liberty —it seems to me that all this patriotism—all this philanthropy—all this religion—appeals to us in favor of the addition of Texas to our Union.

George Bancroft, the eminent historian, into politics up to his neck, was running for governor of Massachusetts on the Democratic ticket. At a mass rally he tried to unite northerners of all classes behind the demand for expansion, showing them that each had much to gain by the taking of all Oregon:

For the vindication of our territory in its full extent, the merchants, and manufacturers, and agriculturists are equally interested. The harbors of Oregon are for American ships; its markets for American labor; its soil for the American ploughs; its wide domain for American institutions and American independence.

Those on the other side of this issue were not quiet. A renewed clamor arose against Texas annexation. A strong influence was *Thoughts on the Evils of a Spirit of Conquest, and on Slavery; A Letter on the Annexation of Texas to the United States,* written by William Ellery Channing, the eminent Boston divine. He tried to make the country think through the implications of expansionist policy:

Wars with Europe and Mexico are to be entailed on us by the annexation of Texas. And is war the policy by which this country is to flourish? Was it for interminable conflicts that we formed our Union? Is it blood shed for plunder, which is to consolidate our institutions? . . . Is it by arming ourselves against the moral sentiments of the world, that we are to build up national honor? Must we of the North buckle on our armor, to fight the battles of slavery, to fight for a possession, which our moral principles and just jealousy forbid us to incorporate with our confederacy?

The Vermont legislature had already adopted a resolution against the annexation of Texas, or of "any state whose constitution tolerates domestic slavery." So now did the legislatures of Massachusetts, Ohio, Rhode Island, and Michigan.

Clay ran scared when he saw the appeal of Polk's expansionist platform. Now the Whig candidate said he "would be glad to see Texas admitted on fair terms." As for slavery, it "ought not to affect the question one way or another."

Clay's tightrope dance caused abolitionist Whigs in New York and Michigan to switch their votes from him to the Liberty party's antislavery candidate, James A. Birney. Polk won—a narrow victory; his popular vote was 1,338,464 against 1,300,097 for Clay. The Liberty party vote that went to Birney had turned the balance for Polk.

Four months stood in between Polk's election in November and his inauguration in March. President Tyler, declaring the election's outcome a popular mandate for immediate annexation, put before Congress a joint resolution for the incorporation of Texas into the Union. (Recall that earlier Tyler had failed to get the two-thirds vote in the Senate needed for a treaty of annexation.) By taking this course, he needed only a simple majority.

The opposition was furious. It pointed out that there was no popular majority for annexation. Add Clay's vote to the 62,300 votes cast for Birney and you had a total that exceeded Polk's vote. Still, Tyler, perhaps bent on chalking up some historic deed before his departure, maneuvered passage of the resolution. He signed it on March 1, three days before he left the White House.

"Who's the next customer," asked the *New York Morning News*, "California or Canada?"

That year, to the tune of "Lucy Neale," Americans who supported the taking of Texas and Oregon were singing the new "Song of Texas."

The Song of Texas

I fear no haugh-ty na-tion, Though foes all 'round are piled, For __ now I take my sta-tion As __ Un-cle Sam-my's child.

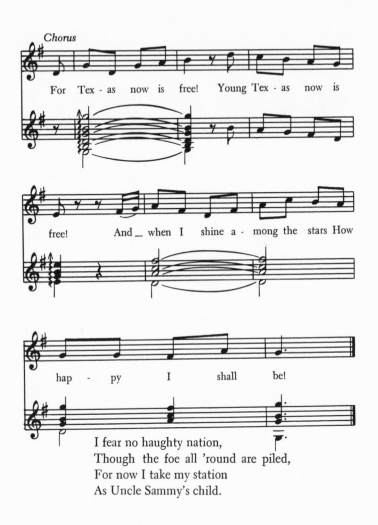

For Tex - as now is free! Young Tex - as now is

free! And — when I shine a - mong the stars How

hap - py I shall be!

I fear no haughty nation,
Though the foe all 'round are piled,
For now I take my station
As Uncle Sammy's child.

For Texas now is free!
Young Texas now is free!
And when I shine among the stars
How happy I shall be!

Though Mexico in pride now,
Begins to threaten blows,
I'll grin at Sammy's side now,
With my thumb upon my nose.

CHORUS

In thirty-six I was of age,
Took Liberty's degrees,
And to unite I have a right,
With any state I please

CHORUS

In Liberty's pure laws, now,
Uncle Sam and I are one,
And I will aid his cause, now,
For Sister Oregon.

CHORUS

With Freedom's fire prolific,
We'll clear our rightful bound,
From Atlantic to Pacific
Is Uncle Sam's own ground.

The whole shall yet be free,
The whole shall yet be free,
And Uncle Sam shall have it all
In peace and Liberty.

5

GOD'S FINGER POINTS

Still in a hurry, on the night of March 3, 1845—his last day in office—President Tyler sent instructions to the American chargé in Texas, ordering him to arrange for immediate annexation.

The next morning James Polk took office.

The new president was not in such a hurry. In charge now, he meant to do things his way. He promptly sent word to Texas to hold off on Tyler's directive. Then he formed his cabinet and asked their advice on Texas. They liked Tyler's speedy action. So out went another directive, offering Texas immediate annexation. There was wild enthusiasm among the settlers. It only remained for the Lone Star Republic to go through the legal motions. Before the year was up, Texas became a state.

Young John O'Sullivan, now running the *New York Morning News* as well as his magazine, tossed his hat in the air. "More! More! More!" he shouted in a *News* editorial. "Yes, more, more, more till our national destiny is fulfilled and . . . the whole boundless continent is ours." In his *Democratic Review* for July–August 1845, justifying the move on Texas, he at last gave history his much-quoted phrase: "The fulfillment of our manifest destiny [is] to overspread the continent allotted by Providence for the free development of our yearly multiplying millions. . . ."

Then O'Sullivan cast his eye on California:

California will, probably, next fall away from the loose adhesion which, in such a country as Mexico, holds a remote province in a slight equivocal kind of dependence on the metropolis. Imbecile and distracted, Mexico can never exert the real governmental authority over such a country. The impotence of the one and the distance of the other, must make the relation one of virtual independence. . . .

A population will soon be in actual occupation of California, over which it will be idle for Mexico to dream of dominion. They will necessarily become independent. All this without agency of our government, without responsibility of our people—in the natural flow of events, the spontaneous working of principles, and the adaptation of the tendencies and wants of the human race to the elemental circumstances in the midst of which they find themselves placed.

Toward the end, O'Sullivan's belligerent words suggested that Britain had better prepare to defend Canada from the American expansionists:

Away, then, with all idle French talk of balances of power on the American Continent. There is no growth in Spanish America! Whatever progress of population there may be in the British Canadas, is only for their own early severance of their present colonial relations to the little island three thousand miles across the Atlantic;

John L. O'Sullivan.

soon to be followed by Annexation, and destined to swell the still accumulating momentum of our progress. And whosoever may hold the balance, though they should cast into the opposite scale all the bayonets and cannon, not only of France and England, but of Europe entire, how would it kick the beam against the simple solid weight of the two hundred and fifty or three hundred millions—and American millions—destined to gather beneath the flutter of the stripes and stars, in the fast hastening year of the Lord 1945!

Polk also pleased the expansionists by making a bold claim on Oregon. In his inaugural address he said, "Our title to the country of Oregon is 'clear and unquestionable,' and already are our people preparing to perfect that title by occupying it with their wives and children."

In reality, only a fraction of the huge Oregon territory was in dispute. That part below the Columbia River the British were not claiming seriously. The Americans, wanting Puget Sound as a harbor, had many times before offered to settle for an extension of the 49th parallel to the Pacific. And Polk, a southerner, was more concerned about the Southwest than the Northwest. So while he talked tough about his readiness to go to war over the Oregon claims, he arranged a peaceful settlement with Britain. The United States acquired Oregon up to the 49th parallel. The British kept all of Vancouver Island and the right to navigate the Columbia River. The Senate quickly approved the treaty, 41 to 14.

That compromise settlement—fair though it seems—made political trouble for Polk in the Northwest. He had shouted "Fifty-four Forty or Fight!" and now he settled for a lot less. A cowardly "sellout," the expansionists said. "All of Texas and All of Oregon"? All of Texas, yes; there *slave* territory would be acquired and Mexico was weak. All of Oregon, no; there *free* territory was involved and Britain was strong.

With the Oregon issue out of the way, Polk could concentrate on Mexico. When the Congress offered annexation to Texas, Mexico reacted promptly and angrily. Back in November 1843, Mexico had warned that if the United States should "commit the unheard-of aggression" of seizing "an integral part of Mexican territory," Mexico would declare war. When President Tyler signed the resolution for Texas annexation, Mexico did not go that far but broke off diplomatic relations at once.

Polk decided to make a direct approach to Mexico. In the fall of 1845 he sent John Slidell, a Louisiana expansionist, to Mexico with a secret offer to purchase California for $25 million, New Mexico for $5 million, and an agreement to assume the claims American citizens had on Mexico. Polk felt the price didn't matter: he was prepared to go as high as $40 million. But poor as Mexico was, how could any politician hope to survive the sale of half his country's land at any price?

The boundary between Texas and Mexico had long been in dispute. When Texas was part of Mexico, its boundary had run along the Nueces River. Several maps published in the U.S. showed this river as the boundary. But once it declared its independence, Texas claimed a boundary some 200 miles to the west, along the Rio Grande, on the disputed theory that the river had been the southern boundary of the Louisiana Purchase. Texas troops had never occupied the land between the two

WAR! OR NO WAR

Ike! say the 49th & lets settle it amercably

No Sir = ree Igoes for the hull of Oregon or none. — I do & don't do nor thin else

Street discussion in New York about the settlement of the Oregon question; 1846 lithograph.

rivers. Texas may have claimed the Rio boundary as a bargaining counter to be used in future negotiations with Mexico.

Another issue between the two powers was the claims by American citizens against Mexico arising from the repeated revolutions. Foreign investors insisted Mexico should be accountable for the claims that usually pile up when a country undergoes such upheavals. In 1839, after long negotiations, arbitration reduced the much padded claims to about $2 million. Mexico paid some installments, but stopped when her treasury went bankrupt. This default was held by some to be a breach of faith.

At the time that Polk sent Slidell to Mexico to see if he could make a deal on these issues, what was the situation inside Mexico?

A struggle for control of Mexico had been going on ever since the revolt against Spain had been won in 1821. The liberals were pitted against the conservatives. Strongest in the liberal ranks were the mestizos. They fought to break the power of the ruling class—made up of white landowners, the Catholic Church, and the army. Although these groups had their differences, too, fear of the liberals gaining control served to unite them against the common enemy. The conservatives wanted to keep Mexico as it had been—themselves in command and the mestizos and Indians underfoot.

Seemingly untouched by this struggle for power was the great mass of the Mexican people. Most of them lived a life of virtual servitude on the haciendas or in the villages. Almost all were illiterate, indifferent to politics, rousing themselves only when a draft into the army threatened them.

The intellectuals who thought about politics sought for ways to shape the country into a nation. Lucas Alamán, a conservative businessman and historian, believed this could best be done by economic organization—by encouraging industry and credit banking, providing mass education, and using power centrally to impose order and provide direction. The liberal historian Lorenzo de Zavala held that Mexico's future lay in awakening the people in the villages from their long sleep by giving them land, freeing them from the clergy, and calling upon them to take part in governing themselves.

Elections were held in Mexico, but only a small percentage of the people were given the right to vote. The strong men of the provinces, called the *caciques,* controlled the elections and made the important decisions. Only in the few cities, where most enfranchised citizens lived, did the electoral process have any meaning. And Mexico City was about the only place where the elections were to some extent free and open.

Strong personalities, then, rather than political parties, were the key forces. The parties as such represented little more than tendencies. They were not at this time true political organizations. The contests for power were waged by bureaucrats, the military, and the intellectuals, working through clubs such as the Masonic lodges which had been imported into Mexico in 1818.

Justo Sierra, a Mexican poet, statesman, and historian writing during the postwar generation, paints a picture of his country as backward, divided, and bankrupt on the eve of the war with the United States. "The opposing parties in Mexico," he wrote, "used the Texas question as a political club, each accusing the other of traitorous intentions." While the United States was holding its election in 1844, a president was also being chosen in Mexico. "But here," says Sierra, "the campaign was strictly military: the guns of civil war took the place of the ballot boxes." The outcome was the assumption of the presidency by General José Joaquin de Herrera. At the beginning of the crucial year, 1845, says Sierra, matters stood thus:

The Congress turned its attention to the American menace, ever more sinister—like a hand gloved in iron clutching the throat of a frail and bloodless nation, like a brutal knee in its belly, like a mouth avid with the desire to bite, to rip, to devour, while prating of humanity, of justice, of law. The government of the patriotic, honest and prudent General Herrera did the best it could, and what it achieved was this: one army on the frontier, another on the way to the frontier, an appeal for unity in the cause of a country threatened with death, an admirable and circumspect dignity with regard to the Americans, but no refusal to compromise or to seek an agreement based on the independence of Texas.

The underlying reality, however, was this: the minority that could think and read, anxious, febrile, critical, shaken incessantly by spasms of bellicose rage which made the government vacillate, clamored for vengeance, yet balked at any self-sacrifice; money was being hidden away; the military were plotting new revolts; the rural masses were inert, ignorant, without affection for the masters who exploited them, without any common spirit, without feeling for their country.

In July President Polk moved General Zachary Taylor,

Sarah Polk's cameo of her husband.

commander of American troops in the Southwest, from Louisiana to Corpus Christi, advising him to prepare to defend Texas against possible Mexican attack. Polk also ordered the navy's Home Squadron to assemble off Mexican ports on the Gulf. Realizing such moves might bring on war, the *Hartford Times* wrote:

If our country is called to a conquest of Mexico, by an unprovoked commencement of hostilities on her part, we shall believe the call is from heaven; that we are called to redeem from unhallowed hands a land above all others, favored of heaven, and to hold it for the use of a people who know how to obey heaven's behests.

Herrera and other Mexican leaders, says Sierra,

understood by now that annexation must be accepted as an historical fact; the important thing was to save, if we could, the rest of our imperiled land. But the pressure of public opinion, violent in its unreasoning emotion, thwarted the delicate adjustments of diplomacy. What was needed in this emergency was not a people sick with distorted imaginings, with hatred and with poverty, but a robust, self-controlled people who would give our ministers leeway to dispel with artful correspondence the formidable danger that loomed over us.

Herrera was willing to see the new American minister, but when Slidell landed in Vera Cruz the opposition was shouting for war. Meanwhile Polk had secretly instructed the American minister in California that should the Californians "desire to unite their destiny with ours, they will be received as brethren." In other words, Polk would support any movement for separation from Mexico.

Hard pressed by his internal enemies, Herrera tried to save himself by shifting position. Now he said he would receive no minister from the United States until Texas was returned to Mexico. His foreign minister, Manuel de la Peña y Peña, hoping to avert war, wrote:

War with the United States in order to dislodge the occupation of Texas is an abyss without bottom which will devour an indefinite series of generations and treasure which the imagination is unable to calculate and in the end will submerge the republic with all its hopes for the future.

His warning went unheard. General Mariano Paredes y Arrilliga, who had been sent to repel an American invasion, charged that Herrera's government was betraying the country. Paredes revolted in December 1845 and overthrew Herrera.

When Polk heard that the Mexicans had refused to see Slidell, and that Herrera's government had fallen, he ordered Taylor to the north bank of the Rio Grande with this instruction:

It is not designed in our present relations with Mexico that you should treat her as an enemy; but should she assume that character by a declaration of war, or any open act of hostility towards us, you will not act merely on the defensive, if your relative means enable you to do otherwise.

An assembly of persons appointed by himself made Paredes president of Mexico. He then discarded the constitution as "of no use" and convoked a constituent assembly. In Sierra's view these were Mexico's chances:

Of no use was the army, debased into an instrument of cynical ambitions; of no use was the middle class, cowardly, fawning and self-seeking; of no use was the clergy, who considered themselves more important than their country and spent their zeal safeguarding their riches, and, although they could boast men of exemplary Christian virtue, these only served as contrast to the mass of ignorant, superstitious, and corrupt monks. The only element that was of any use was the people, who were ruthlessly exploited by all the others.

Nevertheless, many Mexicans thought they could win a war with the United States. They believed in the justice of their cause, and they saw the Americans as greedy, aggressive, and evil. They were ready to defend their homeland from attack. They knew their government was not stable, but their army was four times bigger than the Americans'. They took Whig and antislavery opposition to the war to mean deep unrest in the United States that would damage morale. And some hoped that the war would spark a slave revolt that would keep the American army busy putting down the blacks.

6

OUR COUNTRY, RIGHT OR WRONG?

At the head of his small army of four thousand men, General Taylor marched to the Rio Grande. Across the countryside his soldiers scattered a proclamation written in Spanish:

Your government is in the hands of tyrants and usurpers. We come to obtain indemnity for the past and security for the future . . . we come to overthrow the tyrants who have destroyed your liberties; but we come to make no war upon the people of Mexico, nor upon any form of free government they may choose for themselves. . . .

When he reached the Rio Grande Taylor positioned his cannon to command Matamoros, on the opposite side, and to blockade the river. The effect was to stop supplies from reaching the Mexican army by sea.

Polk hoped Taylor's army, camped in the disputed territory, would provoke the Mexican generals to attack the Americans. But a month passed with no military action. The impatient President began to draft a message asking Congress for a declaration of war upon Mexico.

The chief reason, he said, was the rejection of the Slidell mission.

On April 25, 1846 Mexican cavalry crossed the Rio Grande above Taylor's camp. Learning of this move, Taylor sent dragoons in their direction. The Mexicans intercepted and surrounded the dragoons, who failed to fight their way out. After several of their men were killed, the Americans surrendered. General Taylor at once sent a dispatch to his government saying that "hostilities may now be considered as commenced."

As yet unaware of these events, on Saturday, May 9, Polk told his cabinet that although he had no news of "an open act of aggression by the Mexican army," there was ample cause for war. His war message was ready and would be sent to Congress. The excuse for war—that Mexico had refused to negotiate with Slidell—did not seem strong enough to Secretary of the Navy George Bancroft. He said he would be happier if the government would delay action until Mexico would fire the first shot. Then the war could be presented as a defensive one, and the people would be sure to unite behind it.

The door had scarcely closed upon the departing cabinet when the "good news" arrived from General Taylor: Mexico had fired the useful shot. Polk called the cabinet together again. They voted unanimously that he should send a war message to Congress on Monday, May 11.

Polk spent the Sabbath hurriedly reworking his message. He still listed the old grievances against Mexico, but now made the skirmish the heart of his case:

We have tried every effort at reconciliation. The cup

General Taylor defeating the Mexicans,
as shown in an 1846 caricature.

of forbearance had been exhausted even before the recent information from the frontier of the Del Norte [Rio Grande]. But now, after reiterated menaces, Mexico has passed the boundary of the United States, has invaded our territory and shed American blood upon the American soil. She has proclaimed that hostilities have commenced, and that the two nations are now at war.

As war exists, and, notwithstanding all our efforts to avoid it, exists by the act of Mexico herself, we are called upon by every consideration of duty and patriotism to vindicate with decision the honor, the rights, and the interests of our country. . . .

In further vindication of our rights and defense of our territory, I invoke the prompt action of Congress to recognize the existence of the war, and to place at the disposition of the Executive the means of prosecuting the war with vigor, and thus hastening the restoration of peace.

At noon on Monday Congress sat to receive the President's message. With it came a war bill appropriating $10 million and authorizing the President to call out 50,000 volunteers. "Only two hours for debate," ruled the Democratic majority; they then used up three-fourths of that time by reading excerpts from documents said to support Polk's message. When Whigs demanded a day to study the documents, they were refused it. Toward the end of the allotted time, a Polk man added a preamble to the supply bill declaring that "By the act of the Republic of Mexico a state of war exists between that government and the United States." This forced the members either to approve Polk's position that the war was defensive, or to vote down the money and men requested to save Taylor's army from being destroyed.

The expansionists cheered Polk's move. Opponents of the war—and they included not only Whigs but also such Democrats as Calhoun—tried desperately to gain time to organize a peace coalition but the Democratic machine shoved the bill through ruthlessly. Congressmen who asked for the floor to protest were invisible to the Speaker. Using a parliamentary trick, Kentucky Whig Garrett Davis broke through the gag on debate to "protest solemnly against defiling the measure with the unfounded statement that Mexico began this war. . . . The river Nueces is the true western boundary of Texas. . . . It is our own President who began this war."

The administration leaders excused their haste on the ground that Taylor's army was outnumbered and in danger of being destroyed. Haste was vital. Not true, said the opposition. Taylor already had the help of militia from the neighboring states. And if he really were in peril, help from Washington could never arrive on time.

But Polk's stampede worked. The House was forced to vote on the bill two hours after it was introduced. It passed, 174 to 14. New England, led by John Quincy Adams, supplied most of the negative votes, with 5 nays coming from Ohio. Congressmen against the war but with less courage than the nay-sayers abstained from voting—25 northern and 10 southern (22 Democrats and 13 Whigs).

The next day the administration's men twisted the Senate's arm in the same way. Less than one day was permitted for debate. Whigs rose to demand the "false" preamble be struck from the bill. Clayton of Delaware said that when the President had given Taylor his orders he had committed an act of war without consulting Congress. Calhoun, the southern Democrat, joined the Whigs. More important than the question of the real aggressor, he said, was the question of whether a little skirmish at the Rio Grande constituted war.

When the Senate voted on the war bill there were 40 who said aye and only 2—Clayton of Delaware and John Davis of Massachusetts—who said nay. Abstentions accounted for 3 senators, including Calhoun, while 11 senators were absent.

"The passing of the war bill," wrote Polk's biographer, Charles G. Sellers, "was a striking demonstration of a determined President's ability to compel a reluctant Congress to support a jingoistic foreign policy."

Just as in the House, the Senate vote was deceptive on the true amount of opposition. Many who were against the war, and even spoke up, in the end voted aye. Why? Horace Greeley, in his *New York Tribune* of May 12, had one explanation. Calling his editorial "Our Country, Right or Wrong!" he wrote:

This is the spirit in which a portion of the Press, which admits that our treatment of Mexico has been ruffianly and piratical, and that the invasion of her territory by Gen. Taylor is a flagrant outrage, now exhorts our People to rally in all their strength, to lavish their blood and treasure in the vindictive prosecution of War on Mexico. We protest against such counsel. . . .

We can easily defeat the armies of Mexico, slaughter them by thousands, and pursue them perhaps to their

Horace Greeley.

capital; we can conquer and "annex" their territory; but what then? Have the histories of the ruin of Greek and Roman liberty consequent on such extensions of empire by the sword no lesson for us? Who believes that a score of victories over Mexico, the "annexation" of half her provinces, will give us more Liberty, a purer Morality, a more prosperous Industry, than we now have? . . . Is not Life miserable enough, comes not Death soon enough, without resort to the hideous enginery of War?

People of the United States! Your Rulers are precipitating you into a fathomless abyss of crime and calamity! Why sleep you thoughtless on the verge, as though this was not your business, or Murder could be hid from the sight of God by a few flimsy rags called banners? Awake and arrest the work of butchery ere it shall be too late to preserve your souls from the guilt of wholesale slaughter!

A handful of the minority did try to carry out their constitutional duty. One of them was Joshua Giddings, a frontier lawyer with the torso and temper of a fighting bull. He had been old man Adams's strong right arm in the big contest over the right of petition. He had championed the cause of the Indians and their black allies in the recent Seminole War. And when Congress had censured him for condemning American efforts to seize and try the mutinous slaves from the vessel *Creole*, he had resigned his seat and been triumphantly reelected. Now, a maverick as always, Giddings told the House:

This war is waged against an unoffending people, without just or adequate cause, for the purposes of conquest; with the design to extend slavery; in violation of the

Constitution, against the dictates of justice, of humanity, the sentiments of the age in which we live, and the precepts of the religion we profess. I will lend it no aid, no support whatever. I will not bathe my hands in the blood of the people of Mexico, nor will I participate in the guilt of those murders which have been, and which will hereafter be committed by our army there. For these reasons I shall vote against the bill under consideration, and all others calculated to support this war.

Later, Calhoun said that if allowed time to examine the documents, 90 percent of the Congress would have voted nay on the war bill. When he did get a chance to read the documents about the Slidell mission, Senator Frank Blair of Maryland remarked that Polk "has got to lying in public as well as private." Charles Francis Adams (son of John Quincy), called the war bill's preamble "one of the grossest national lies that was ever deliberately told."

Men like Senator John A. Dix of New York confided to friends that they would have voted against the "Texas fraud" but didn't because they feared the charge of "high treason." Stephen A. Douglas of Illinois, who would later become a senator and national leader of the Democratic party, was quick to apply that label. To Congressman Delano of Ohio, who attacked the war as "unholy, unrighteous and damnable," Douglas replied, "Is there not treason in the heart that can feel, and poison in the breath that can utter, such sentiments against their own country, when forced to take up arms in self-defense, to repel the invasion of a brutal and perfidious foe?"

Now Polk had his war, a war he knew would start with public support. Months before, the *New York Herald* had said, "The multitude cry aloud for war." And the *New York Morning News* echoed, "Nine-tenths of our people . . . would rather have a little fighting than not." "Let us go to war," wrote the *New York Journal of Commerce*. "The world has become stale and insipid, the ships ought to be all captured, and the cities battered down, and the world burned up, so that we can start again. There would be fun in that. Some interest—something to talk about."

When news of American blood shed by Mexicans arrived, such feelings caught fire. On May 11, the day the House voted for the war bill, the poet Walt Whitman, then twenty-seven, wrote in the *Brooklyn Eagle*:

Yes; Mexico must be thoroughly chastised! We have reached a point in our intercourse with that country, when prompt and effectual demonstrations of force are enjoined upon us by every dictate of right and policy. The news of yesterday has added the last argument wanted to prove the necessity of an immediate Declaration of War by our government toward its southern neighbor.

Even in Ohio's Western Reserve, abolitionist country, one of Giddings' friends had to report that, like Whitman, the people "are sadly inclined to Huzza for the Mexican war."

A call for enlistees went out on May 15, with quotas set for each state and community. "Mexico or Death" posters appeared on walls everywhere. In Illinois fourteen regiments enrolled, although only four had been

VOLUNTEERS !

Men of the Granite State!

Men of Old Rockingham!! the

strawberry-bed of patriotism, renowned for bravery and devotion to Country, rally at this call. Santa Anna, reeking with the generous confidence and magnanimity of your countrymen, is in arms, eager to plunge his traitor-dagger in their bosoms. To arms, then, and rush to the standard of the fearless and gallant CUSHING----put to the blush the dastardly meanness and rank toryism of Massachusetts. Let the half civilized Mexicans hear the crack of the unerring New Hampshire rifleman, and illustrate on the plains of San Luis Potosi, the fierce, determined, and undaunted bravery that has always characterized her sons.

Col. THEODORE F. ROWE, at No. 31 Daniel-street, is authorized and will enlist men this week for the Massachusetts Regiment of Volunteers. The compensation is $10 per month---$30 in advance. Congress will grant a handsome bounty in money and ONE HUNDRED AND SIXTY ACRES OF LAND.

Portsmouth, Feb. 2. 1847.

Mexican War recruiting poster.

called for. In Tennessee 30,000 men appeared when 3,000 were requested. Kentucky had to close enlistments in ten days because volunteers were so numerous. Of the 70,000 who would volunteer for the Mexican war, 40,000 would enlist from the states of the great Mississippi Valley, only 8,000 from the Northern states. The more remote men were from the scene of the war, the less inclined they were to volunteer.

The day Polk signed the war bill, Park Benjamin, popular poet and journalist, scribbled new words to the tune of "A Wet Sheet and a Flowing Sea." Called "To Arms!" it was soon being sung by the troops in Taylor's army.

To Arms!

A - wake A - rise! Ye men of might! The glo - rious hour is nigh. Your ea - gle paus - es in high flight And screams his bat - tle cry! From North to South, from East to West, Send back an an - swering cheer, And say fare - well to peace and rest, And ban - ish doubt and fear!

Chorus

Arm! Arm! Your coun - try bids you arm! Fling out your ban - ners free. Let drum and trum - pet sound a - larm, O'er moun - tain plain and sea.

Awake! Awake! Ye men of might!
The glorious hour is nigh.
Your eagle pauses in high flight
And screams his battle cry!
From North to South, from East to West,
Send back an answering cheer,
And say farewell to peace and rest,
And banish doubt and fear!

CHORUS:
Arm! Arm! Your country bids you arm!
Fling out your banners free.
Let drum and trumpet sound alarm,
O'er mountain, plain and sea.

To kindred of the noble dead,
As noble deeds should dare;
The fields whereon their blood was shed
A deeper stain must wear.
To arms! To arms! Ye men of might!
Away from home, away!
The first and foremost in the fight
Are sure to win the day!

CHORUS

FUN AND FROLIC

The volunteer companies of the Midwest poured down the tributaries into the Mississippi and out onto the Gulf of Mexico. From eastern ports steamers carried other volunteers south on the Atlantic to join forces with Taylor's regulars. They knew little about Mexico or what awaited them on its distant battlefields. As they swarmed confidently southward, to the tune of "Bound to the Rio Grande," all they had was the American cockiness about their ability to fight anyone, anywhere, and win in a hurry.

Part of their self-assurance came from the widespread belief that Mexicans were an inferior people. Indians, half-breeds, blacks—wasn't that what six out of seven Mexicans were? And the other seventh—degenerate Spaniards. As for their army, it was "a feeble and degraded soldiery, who would be scattered like chaff by the first volley from the Anglo-Saxon rifle, the first charge of the Anglo-Saxon bayonet." Against such an opponent, said the *Commercial Bulletin*, a war would be "an adventure full of fun and frolic and holding forth the rewards of opulence and glory."

Until the volunteers arrived, the fighting in Mexico

Bound to the Rio Grande

Guitar introduction

Oh, say, were you ev - er in the Ri - o Grande? Way, you Ri - o! _____ It's there that the ri - ver runs down gol - den sand. For we're bound for the Ri - o

Chorus

Grande. And a - way, you Ri - o!

Way, you Ri - o! Sing fare you well, my

pret - ty young girls For we're bound for the Ri o

Grande!

Oh, say, were you ever in the Rio Grande?
Way, you Rio!
It's there that the river runs down golden sand.
For we're bound to the Rio Grande!

CHORUS:
And away, you Rio!
Way, you Rio!
Sing fare you well,
My pretty young girls,
For we're bound to the Rio Grande!

Oh, New York town is no place for me—
Way, you Rio!
I'll pack up my bag and go to sea.
For we're bound to the Rio Grande!

CHORUS

We'll sell our salt cod for molasses and rum—
Way, you Rio!
And get home again 'fore Thanksgiving has come.
For we're bound to the Rio Grande!

CHORUS

would be in the hands of the regular army. All told, it numbered only 7,200 men. The army had spent far more time on garrison duty than in fighting. Desertions had recently averaged 1,000 a year. Three brigades of the regulars, with about 2,300 men, were under Taylor's command. Their pay was seven dollars a month. Few ambitious civilians would enlist for such a reward when civil life offered far greater opportunities. Promotion in the regular army was closed to the enlisted men. Many of the regulars were of foreign birth—English, Irish, German, French, Polish—and a number had seen action in the Napoleonic wars.

The infantry's standard weapon was the flintlock musket, but a small number of men were equipped with the new percussion-cap musket. The flintlock was charged with paper cartridges packed with powder, buckshot, and ball. The musket could reach targets no more than a few hundred yards off. Army uniforms were blue—a light tone for the enlisted men, dark blue for the officer's frock coats and light blue for their gold-braided trousers.

Federal policy throughout the nineteenth century was to keep only a small regular army. Its duties were to police the borders and put down insurrections. Now, in time of war, the regular army was the core around which the volunteer force would be built. Confident that this war would end swiftly, Washington set only a twelve-month enlistment period for the volunteers, a policy it would bitterly regret.

The regulars were far outnumbered by the volunteers. These raw recruits would have to bear the burden of the fighting. In the critical eye of the West Pointer, the volunteers were an unlovely and unlikely lot. They paid no attention to discipline, were ignorant of the care of equipment, indifferent to proper uniform, careless of weapons, and hostile to routine of any kind. Watching them at a farcical drill, one regular noted the "torn and dirty shirts—uncombed heads—unwashed faces."

But such men turned out to have the same appetite and skill for fighting that Americans had shown since the days of the French and Indian Wars. They knew how to make the most of their weapons. Many had been hunters on the frontier and their marksmanship was superb. They learned how to use light, mobile artillery with smashing effect against the cavalry the Mexicans relied on. Their junior officers, too—a significant percentage of them West Pointers for the first time in the nation's military history—proved a competence in combat that would win them great reputations one day in another war.

Democracy ruled in the volunteer militia companies. The men elected their own officers, and if they didn't like an officer, they were quick to throw him out in favor of another. Not all were prompted to enlist for love of flag and glory. Some signed up to get cash bounties and felt no devotion to a cause. Such men deserted easily and frequently.

Polk and his advisers quickly worked out the basic strategy for the war. They planned a triple thrust against Mexico. An Army of the West would conquer New Mexico and California; an Army of the Center would seize Chihuahua and northern Mexico; and an Army of Occupation would drive south to Mexico City to cap-

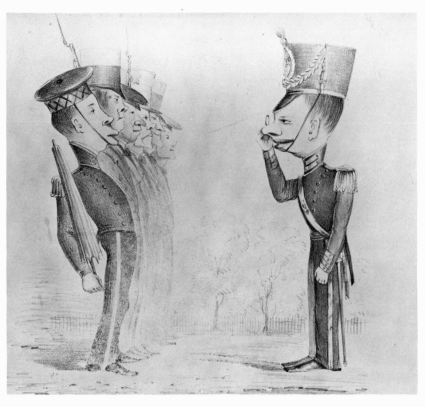

Cartoon of volunteers for Texas, 1846.

ture the capital and conclude the war under terms that would satisfy American ambitions.

The U.S. Navy in the last few years had grown considerably, in spite of some congressional opposition. It had about 11,000 men and nearly 1,000 guns afloat. Its job now would be to blockade the ports on the Gulf of Mexico and along the western coast. Enforcing blockades and ferrying men and supplies were dull chores for naval officers who remembered the great sea battles of the War of 1812.

Polk wanted a short war. One reason for haste was to control California and the Southwest territory before the losses of a more protracted war reduced popular enthusiasm. Another motive was political. The two leading generals—Winfield Scott and Zachary Taylor—happened to be Whigs. Victories would build their popularity and make either one a presidential candidate for the Democrats to fear in the 1848 election, scarcely two years off. So Polk, as Senator Thomas Hart Benton said, "wanted a small war, just large enough to require a treaty of peace, and not large enough to make military reputations dangerous for the presidency."

Without waiting for a grand plan of action, Zachary Taylor had to decide for himself what to do against the Mexican "invaders." General Taylor was sixty-two now, a short man with a thick trunk barreling up from stubby legs. His face was wrinkled and his skin had weathered yellow. He looked like a farmer, not a military hero. He had been born in Virginia and raised in Louisville, Kentucky. Taylor's education was meager; he was trained only to run the family plantation. Later, many of the officers he commanded sneered at his plain mind and slow speech. His reports often had to be recast into "official" English by his staff. But at twenty-four he went into the army as a lieutenant. He fought in the War of 1812, winning fame by standing off an attack of four hundred Indians commanded by the great Tecumseh. After fifteen years of garrison duty in Louisiana and Minnesota, Taylor was promoted to colonel. He saw his next action in the Black Hawk War. Then in 1837 he fought against the Seminoles in Florida, earning a promotion to brigadier general for his victory in the battle of Lake Okeechobee.

"General Taylor never wore uniform but dressed himself entirely for comfort," said Ulysses S. Grant, who served under him as a young lieutenant in Mexico. Taylor usually wore a farmer's straw hat or an old oilcloth cap, dirty pantaloons, and a ragged brown, green, or white coat. Grant said "he moved about the field in which he was operating to see through his own eyes the situation. Often he would be without staff officers, and when he was accompanied by them there was no prescribed order in which they followed. He was very much given to sit his horse sideways—with both feet on one side—particularly on the battlefield."

Taylor was a blunt man, willful, tough, stubborn. He used to say he felt "as honest and good as anybody else." His troops liked him for his coolness in action, and nicknamed him "Old Rough and Ready." He enjoyed swapping stories with his men and had a ready laugh. His temper, however, was notorious. Once he took a dislike to a man, he never gave it up.

One of the many engaging stories about Old Zack appears in the reminiscences of Samuel E. Chamberlain, a volunteer in the Mexican War. This is how he tells it:

When the 1st Virginia Volunteers under Colonel Hamtranck arrived they were as curious as any Yankees to see General Taylor. A certain Lieutenant who prided himself on belonging to one of the first families of the State went up to Headquarters to obtain a glimpse of the General. Seeing an old man cleaning a sword in a bower, the officer went in and with that high-toned dignity which the descendants of Pocahontas and other Virginians are so famous for, addressed the bronze-faced old gentleman who was hard to work in his shirt sleeves, "I say, old fell, can you tell me where I can see General Taylor?"

The old "fell" without raising replied, "Wull, stranger, thar is the old hoss's tent," pointing to the Headquarters.

"Lieutenant, if you please," said the F.F.V. "And so that is the humble abode of the great hero. Can I see him? And by the way, my old trump, whose sword is that you are cleaning?"

"Wull Colonel," replied the old man, "I don't see there is any harm in telling you, seeing's you are an officer. This sword belongs to the General himself."

"Ah! Then this is the victorious blade of the immortal hero! And I suppose then, my worthy man, that you work for the General?"

The worthy man replied, "I reckon, and doggone hard, and little thanks and small pay I get too."

The Lieutenant took off his sword and said, "My good

man, I would like to have you clean my sword, and I shall come tomorrow to see the General and then I will give you a dollar."

The Lieutenant was on hand the next day and seeing his old friend of the day before standing under an awning conversing with some officers, beckoned for him to come out and see him. The old gentleman came out, bringing the Lieutenant's sword. The Lieutenant was profuse in his thanks and giving the old man a poke in the ribs said, "Come, old fatty, show me General Taylor and the dollar is yours."

The "old fatty" drew himself up and said, "Lieutenant! I am General Taylor," and turning slowly round, "and I will take that dollar!"

In 1840 Taylor was put in command of the Army of the Southwest. It was then that he bought a plantation, becoming a slaveholder. From this post he was shifted to the Nueces River as Polk began to play his cards against the Mexicans.

The army that would face the Americans reflected the divisions splitting Mexican society. The mass of the troops were of Indian strains, coming from the most oppressed classes. They were often raw conscripts, poorly trained and equipped. A great gulf separated the rank and file from officers who often got their commissions through influence. Family ties or political connections could catapult a Mexican into high rank, although he might know nothing of the military profession. Many officers won advancement by knowing when to "pronounce"—when to rise against the "ins" and the "outs." When the "outs" became the "ins," the switch earned

Mexican soldier.

a promotion. Led by officers from a class that had always treated them with contempt, the troops were low in morale. Perhaps because of this, the officers preferred combat by artillery and musket, rather than hand-to-hand combat with bayonet.

Nevertheless, Mexican leaders believed their army was better than the American one. Certainly it was bigger: the regular Mexican army was actually four times as large as the American army. Mexican troops had been fighting one another constantly ever since the revolution of 1821. One could conclude from this that thirty-six years of internal struggles must have left Mexico exhausted. But foreign observers believed the experience had made the Mexican military force one of the best in the world.

Bolstering Mexican confidence was the conviction that geography was in their favor. The war would be fought far from American cities. Over such a great distance, how could sufficient supplies reach American armies on time? Mexico could expect to take and hold the offensive while the Americans would have to rely on defense. Even if U.S. troops should manage to penetrate Mexico, how could they wage war effectively over deserts or on barren mountains, against guerrilla resistance, and with ever-lengthening supply lines?

The general who would take charge of Mexico's forces was Santa Anna. "Of all the sly schemers in the history of Mexico," says Professor Ramon E. Ruiz, "Santa Anna was the master." As a sixteen-year-old cadet in the Spanish army, he fought against the Indian revolutionaries led by Father Miguel Hidalgo. In March 1821 he jumped three grades in just twenty-four hours, ending the day as a full colonel. By the age of twenty-eight he was a brigadier general. Justo Sierra, the Mexican historian, speaks of him as "this great comedian, whose soul was sheer vanity and ambition. . . . Three activities engaged his entire political life: making war, raising money, and plotting." Whether he won or lost, the "National Benefactor" (a title he bestowed upon himself) always lived high. "The hardships of the days when Santa Anna was ruler became legendary," says Sierra. "How he squandered money on the army, on his favorites, on the regal pomp of his entourage! He exacted huge sums from the clergy, who paid him grudgingly, in driblets, and forgave him. Everybody forgave him."

Of his one-man rule, established in 1835, Sierra wrote: "A dictatorship that obstructs justice and creates disorder and affords at best a precarious peace is a downright calamity, and that is what Santa Anna's dictatorship quickly became."

The general was notorious, writes Ruiz, for changing sides "as easily and as often as he changed his gaudy uniforms. But he always kept two goals in mind: he wanted to rule and he wanted to stop the liberal movement from changing Mexico."

News from Mexico traveled slowly north. The high-speed printing press had just arrived, but the speed of news-gathering lagged. Telegraph lines were snaking from city to city, but their gaps had to be bridged by any means from railroads and steamships to the pony express and carrier pigeon.

Official Washington was the chief source of war news. It told the capital correspondents what it wanted them to know, and the men sent their reports on to their home papers.

The *New York Evening Post* was one paper that had several correspondents among the military officers engaged in the fighting, but many others came to rely on the New Orleans press for coverage of the war. Closest to Mexico, New Orleans papers were the first in history to assign reporters to the battlefield. The war correspondents sent their dispatches by ship from the coasts of Mexico and Texas.

Because war news was so slow in coming, it took two weeks for Taylor's report of the first skirmish to reach Washington. Even before Polk opened that dispatch, Taylor's troops had fought the Mexicans two more times.

A few days after the defeat of the Americans on April 25, General Arista had taken his troops across the Rio Grande below Matamoros onto territory claimed by the Americans. Taylor decided to get rid of the Mexican "invaders" before they could cut off his supply line. On the afternoon of May 7 he set out to meet the enemy with 2,000 troops, bringing a train of 250 supply wagons. The army moved seven miles that night and the next morning crossed a wide prairie. Ahead lay a ridge of tall mesquite trees that gave the name Palo Alto to the place. Before the woods the Americans saw the Mexicans lined up on a mile-wide front, with cavalry on the right, artillery in the center, and infantry on the left. In between was dry, thick prairie grass, so tall it reached shoulder-height, and needle-pointed at the tips.

Freshwater ponds sparkled in the sun, and Taylor ordered his men to fill up their canteens and water their horses. The wagons were kept in the rear while the army formed into a solid square. Taylor had already given his battle order, voicing "every confidence in his officers and men. If his orders and instructions are carried out, he has no doubt of the result, let the enemy meet him in what numbers he may. He wishes to enjoin upon the battalions of infantry that their main dependence must be in the bayonet."

That last line in Taylor's order—"dependence must be in the bayonet"—pleased Lieutenant William S. Henry, the West Pointer. "It shows the man," he wrote in his diary; "in it you see confidence, and a determination to win the battle at all hazards."

The fighting began with an artillery duel. Taylor had 2 siege guns and 16 batteries manned by 932 artillerists of the regular army. The Mexicans fired when within 700 yards, but their cannons were so ancient and their powder so poor that their copper shot fell short and bounced along the ground. The Americans laughed and ducked or sidestepped to avoid being hit. Brevet Major Samuel Ringgold, commanding a battery of light guns, moved in fast and cannonaded the Mexican lines. The U.S. artillery would prove deadly to the Mexicans all through the war. Lieutenant Henry described how the batteries operated:

The fire of the gallant Ringgold's battery on our right told with deadly effect upon their mass of cavalry; platoons appeared to be mowed down at a time. The two eighteen-pounders carried death and destruction with them. The cavalry soon found it was getting too warm for them, and commenced moving off, by a flank move-

The death of Major Ringgold at Palo Alto.

ment, to the left in a trot, and were tickled into a gallop by a discharge of the eighteens. Their flank movement threatened our train, and was promptly met by the movement of a section of Ringgold's battery under Lieutenant Ridgely. The strength of this body of cavalry was computed at one thousand, and, therefore, was a formidable demonstration. The 5th received them in square, and from the fire of an angle vacated twenty saddles.

Each shot seemed to take effect, and as our men saw the execution, their cries of triumph mingled with the cannon's roar.

The cannonading lasted an hour, then paused, as both generals shifted their forces. Ringgold's battery, earning the name of the "Flying Artillery," pushed toward the Mexican left flank, with the Fourth Infantry and First Brigade supporting it. Suddenly flames crackled over the plain. The guns had set the grass on fire and now a smokescreen separated the two armies. Again Lieutenant Henry reports what he saw:

Lieut. Duncan, under cover of the smoke, conceived and executed a brilliant flank movement on the enemy's right. He advanced with his battery, and suddenly debouched and poured in a galling enfilading fire upon their right flank; it was thrown into the utmost confusion. His shells and shrapnel shot told with murderous effect. At this moment, if a charge had been made, so great was the confusion of the enemy, the whole field would have been swept; but the general felt bound to protect his train and feared any movement which would have laid it open to an attack. As night approached the fire of the enemy slackened, and it ceased on both sides with the setting sun. We had driven the enemy from his position, and forced him to retire. We encamped as victors upon the field of battle. The last rays of the setting sun tinged with a golden light the clouds of battle that hung heavily over the field of carnage; the weary army rested on their arms, and slept sweetly on the prairie grass.

The Mexican casualties were 320 dead and over 400 wounded, while the American loss was small: 5 killed, 43 wounded.

When morning came, the Mexican troops had disappeared. Taylor had won the battle of Palo Alto but had not destroyed the enemy's army.

General Arista had retreated toward the Rio Grande, some seven miles off, where he decided to make another stand on an old dry channel of the river, called the Resaca de la Palma. Banks four feet high would protect his troops, and thick woods could, he thought, cut down the harm done by the dreaded American artillery.

Taylor decided to give immediate battle, and late in the afternoon of May 9, his men filtered through the woods and forced hand-to-hand combat upon the Mexicans. Arista's soldiers fought hard, but when their left flank was turned, said Henry, they "fled in every direction, and many were drowned in their attempts to swim the river." Again the artillery had played a big role, pouring in its bloody fire. Henry was filled with admiration for his commander:

General Taylor was sitting on his horse in the thickest of the fight, with his sword drawn, while the balls were rattling around him. Colonel C—— remarked to him that he was exposing his person very much, and proposed to him to retire a short distance: "Let us ride a little nearer, the balls will fall behind us," was the general's reply.

In the battle of the Resaca the Americans had won another victory. This time 1,200 Mexicans were killed or wounded, but only 150 Americans. Again Taylor did not pursue the fleeing enemy. He let the Mexicans cross the Rio and disappear into the deserts beyond Matamoros.

"It is a glorious fact for the army," said one officer, "that there were no volunteers with us." The regulars were proud they had done it alone. The officers especially, mostly West Pointers, were gratified. Congress had been threatening to abolish the military academy on the ground that it cost the country a lot and gave it little. The victories on the Rio Grande had proved the worth of West Point.

While squads buried the dead of both armies, the Americans rehashed the battles. They had seen how elegantly uniformed the Mexican officers were, but how incapable of command. They gave no leadership to their troops, neglected their welfare, abused their strength. They would march the soldiers thirty or more miles a day, while the American foot soldiers were rarely asked to do more than fifteen. Brave as they were, the Mexican infantrymen could do little with their poor weapons. They hit their target infrequently because their cartridges were so overloaded with powder that the rifles kicked badly, making accurate aim impossible.

The Americans, too, had reason to gripe about deficiencies. Taylor had not been able to cross the river in pursuit of the enemy because the War Department, though asked a year ago, had never provided a pontoon train for such crossings.

For days the stink of the dead hung over the river. As the water subsided, the bodies of Mexican soldiers who had drowned in flight became visible, stuck in the low branches of trees that had been submerged. The corpses broke loose now, and floated downstream where hungry fish devoured them.

When Taylor's army crossed the river at last, Arista had fled Matamoros. News of his defeats shocked Mexico. The Mexican president, General Paredes, had been confident the nation would rally to its defense and beat the invaders off. Arista was blamed for the disaster and replaced by twenty-four-year-old Francisco Mejía, a political general charged with the task of stopping Taylor's army.

In the United States the news of his two victories made Taylor a national hero. Congress voted him two gold medals, and state legislatures offered him swords of honor. He was breveted a major general and given the title of commander of the Army of the Rio Grande. The press shouted his praises: he was acclaimed the new Caesar, the new Napoleon. Thurlow Weed, the prominent Whig, forecast in his *Albany Journal* that Taylor would be the next President of the United States.

8

THEY DIE LIKE DOGS

Back home the civilians might be shouting huzzas for "Old Rough and Ready," but in Mexico his officers and men had turned to criticizing him. Young West Pointers such as George Meade complained that he had "a perfect inability to make use of any information" given him. In their eyes the old veteran was foolish and bumbling, unfit for command of a modern army.

Sitting in Matamoros the army had only occupation duties to attend to. At first, wrote Lieutenant William Henry, all seemed to go well:

The behavior of our army after victory is as highly honorable as the victories themselves. In taking possession of Matamoros we have not interfered with either the civil or religious rights of the inhabitants. Their courts of justice are still held, the most perfect respect is paid to law and order, and every infraction of either is severely punished. The army, instead of entering the city as conquerors, encamp quietly in the suburbs. Instead of taking possession of their houses for our men, we remain under miserable canvas, which afford no protection from the storm, and scarcely shade to protect the soldier from the noonday sun. Many have no tents, and yet, under these circumstances, no building is occupied: those taken for storehouses and public offices are regularly rented. By such conduct we have restored confidence to the people; the citizens mingle freely among us, walk through our camp, and feel sure of protection. Such conduct should make our countrymen proud of their army.

Lieutenant Henry was so taken with Mexico he began to feel it was a shame that it belonged to the Mexicans:

It certainly never was intended this lovely land, rich in every production, with a climate that exceeds any thing the imagination can conceive of, should remain in the hands of an ignorant and degenerate race. The finger of Fate points, if not to their eventual extinction, to the time when they will cease to be owners, and when the Anglo-American race will rule with republican simplicity and justice, a land literally "flowing with milk and honey." . . . No part of Texas surpasses in fertility, or equals in salubrity, the valley of the Rio Grande. . . . Cultivation can be carried on by white labor, I think, beyond a doubt. No summer climate can exceed it in loveliness; the everlasting breeze deprives the sun of much of its heat. Such evenings! Such a morn! Young people should come here to make love; the old should emigrate and rejuvenate themselves.

But that lyrical mood did not last long. Lack of action led the army into boredom, grumbling, and discontent. Gambling joints, saloons, dance halls, and bordellos opened up as American operators swarmed in from the States to make a killing out of alleviating the troops' boredom. Even vaudeville, the popular form of American theater, was imported to entertain the troops. Joseph Jefferson, the young actor who would later make a great reputation in the role of Rip Van Winkle, was in the company that played to soldiers, settlers, and gamblers in the old Spanish opera house. "We acted to the most motley group that ever filled a theater," he wrote, "a rag tag and bobtail crowd that always followed in the train of an army."

Discipline ran down while the occupation rate of the jails and guardhouses ran up. Now the volunteers were coming off the steamers which had churned their way down to the Gulf. Lieutenant Henry saw the new men were not doing so well:

They have suffered a great deal at their encampments near the mouth of the river. Diarrhea, dysentery, and fevers have been very fatal. They must suffer much more than the regulars, for they have no idea how to collect around them those nameless comforts the old soldier always has; besides, campaigning is entirely out of their line.

"The volunteers continue to pour in," wrote Lieutenant George Gordon Meade to his wife, "and I regret to say I do not see it with much satisfaction." Meade, a West Pointer in the artillery, was appalled by the behavior of the newcomers:

They are perfectly ignorant of discipline, and most restive under restraint. They are in consequence a most

Entertainment for occupation troops in Mexico.

disorderly mass, who will give us, I fear, more trouble than the enemy.

There were volunteers from the upper classes too. They looked no better to Meade. "Gentlemen from Louisiana," he said, "owning plantations and Negroes, come here as common soldiers, and then revolt at the idea of drawing their own water and cutting their own wood and in fact, they expect the regulars, who have to take care of themselves, to play waiter to them."

All summer long the volunteer encampments spread down both sides of the river. Over 20,000 men filled them. Their regiments gave themselves such names as the Guards, the Gunmen, and the Killers. The men tricked themselves out in a vivid variety of costumes. Command gave little thought to providing food or equipment suitable for a climate where heat of 120 degrees was common. Rations meant pork and beans, coffee and hard biscuits. There were no vegetables. The men rustled cattle to get fresh meat and went shrimping on the river for a change of diet. The Rio offered the only drinking water, a blend of sand and mud. Bedtime was night-fighting against sand, flies, chiggers, and mosquitoes.

The chief occupation became watching your comrades die of disease and wondering when your turn would come. Did the men remember now the posters that had enticed them to enlist?

HERE'S TO OLD ZACK!
GLORIOUS TIMES!
ROAST BEEF, ICE CREAM, AND
THREE MONTHS' ADVANCE!

Taylor finally moved the army upriver to Camargo. The new campsite turned out to be no healthier. Rock walls rose on all sides to make the place an oven. Again the young officers had reason to rail against General Taylor. Lieutenant George B. McClellan said, "I have seen more suffering since I came out here than I could have imagined to exist. I allude to the sufferings of the volunteers. They literally die like dogs."

Another young officer, Lew Wallace, lieutenant of Indiana volunteers (later to write the best-selling novel, *Ben-Hur*), said:

I cannot recall another instance of a command so wantonly neglected and so brutally mislocated. . . . The soldier may have been in perfect health the day he went into camp. . . . At rollcall, three weeks having passed, I notice the change in his appearance. His cheeks have the tinge of old gunny sacks; under the jaw the skin is ween and flabby; his eyes are filmy and sinking; he moves listlessly; the voice answering the sergeant is flat; instead of supporting the gun at order arms, the gun is supporting him. . . . The surgeon gives him an opium pill. . . . Another week and his place in the ranks is vacant. A messmate answers for him. . . . There is no hospital of any kind. It will go hard with him, one of six in a close tent, nine feet by nine, for the night will not bring him enough of blessed coolness to soothe the fever made burning through the day. His comrades themselves sick are his nurses. They do their best, but their best is wanting. . . . At last he has no vigor left; mind and will are down together; the final stage is come.

The toll was terrible. Fifteen hundred men died in

the camps at Camargo. Burials went on day and night and the sound of the dead march beat through the air so steadily it was said the mockingbirds learned to whistle the tune. Thievery, rape, and murder became routine under such desperate conditions. Having no enemy to fight, the volunteers fought each other or the Mexican civilians.

Lieutenant Meade, although he admired Taylor as "a brave old man who knows not what fear is," was not blind to Taylor's weaknesses as a commanding general:

Among his most prominent defects is the entire and utter ignorance of the use to which the staff department can be put, and especially my own corps. Did he have his own way, we should be perfectly useless; not from any unfriendly feeling on his part towards us, but from absolute ignorance of what we can be required to do, and perfect inability to make any use of the information we do obtain. He has, however, with him some few officers upon whose judgment he relies, and they every now and then manage to argue him into employing us. Let one fact illustrate this. We arrived at our camp opposite Matamoros on the 28th of March; we broke it up on the 1st of May, remaining there one whole month. During this time, from the commencement to the end, my individual efforts were repeatedly made, as well as were those of other officers, to induce him to reflect upon the subject of bridges, and in the absence of a pontoon train, which Congress was debating about giving us, to call upon his engineer officers for plans for crossing the river with such materials as were at hand. All of us were ready to give our ideas, and to make the

Zachary Taylor and his staff.

necessary preparations and experiments; but, no, the old gentleman would never listen or give it a moment's attention.

As the news of what was happening trickled up to the States, it fueled the growing anger against the war. Most people had accepted the war once the shooting started. But over the summer of 1846 the mood began to shift. Polk was not the kind of President who could inspire the people to feverish enthusiasm for anything. He was too harsh, too sour, too dull to make a magnetic war leader. The abolitionists, who from the beginning had resisted the war on moral grounds, spoke to more receptive ears. Some religious groups too—the Quakers, the Unitarians, the Congregationalists—had all along opposed the war. The preacher William Henry Channing had even said that if he had to fight in this "damnable war," it would be on the side of the Mexicans.

"What shall we do in regard to this present war?" asked another preacher, Theodore Parker. Among Boston's conservatives, the thirty-six-year-old clergyman was notorious for his unorthodox beliefs. But his congregation kept growing until now it had 7,000 members. In 1846 he preached a sermon answering the great question of the day, and linking slavery to the Mexican issue, said:

We can refuse to take any part in it; we can encourage others to do the same; we can aid men, if need be, who suffer because they refuse. Men will call us traitors; what then? That hurt nobody in '76. We are a rebellious nation; our whole history is treason; our blood was attainted before we were born; our creeds are infidelity to the mother church; our constitution treason to our fatherland. What of that? Though all the governors of the world bid us commit treason against man, and set the example, let us never submit. Let God only be a master to control our conscience.

On June 17, 1846, the *Boston Courier* carried a bitter attack on the war called the "Biglow Papers." They were anonymous verses in Yankee dialect. Their effect was instantaneous and explosive. The verses were read, reprinted, copied, quoted. Men stuck them on the walls of their shops to read them while at work. When they appeared in book form, fifteen hundred copies were sold in the first week. Soon everyone learned that the "Biglow Papers" were from the pen of James Russell Lowell, twenty-seven-year-old son of a distinguished family. He won national fame when he let Hosea Biglow voice the feelings of thousands that summer:

> Wut's the use o' meetin'-goin'
> Every Sabbath, wet or dry,
> Ef it's right to go amowin'
> Feller-men like oats an' rye?
> I dunno but wut it's pooty
> Trainin' round in bobtail coats,—
> But it's curus Christian dooty
> This 'ere cuttin' folks's throats.

One evening that July, a year after he had gone to live in a hut by Walden Pond, in Concord, Massachusetts, Henry David Thoreau was put in jail for refusing to pay his poll tax. He had stopped paying the tax four years earlier because he was not willing to support a government that sanctioned slavery, one that he believed had now begun a war with Mexico for the purpose of extending slavery to new territory.

Thoreau spent only one night in jail, and this led to his most influential essay, "The Duty of Civil Disobedience." It was immediately concerned with the Mexican War and the slavery struggle, but it had a universal appeal because it spoke to the issue of the moral law in conflict with the civil law:

Government is at best but an expedient; but most governments are usually, and all governments are sometimes, inexpedient. . . . The government itself, which is only the mode which the people have chosen to execute their will, is . . . liable to be abused and perverted before the people can act through it. Witness the present Mexican War, the work of comparatively a few individuals using the standing government as their tool; for, in the outset, the people would not have consented to this measure. . . . This people must cease to hold slaves, and to make war on Mexico, though it cost them their existence as a people.

Thoreau spoke for more than himself. The legislature in Massachusetts had already urged "all good citizens to join the efforts to arrest this war." In New Hampshire, John P. Hale called the war "unparalleled in infamy in modern history" and introduced a resolution against it which both houses approved and the governor signed.

The most significant opposition grew day by day within the Whig party. North and South the Whigs had

Typical militia drill of the Mexican war period.

been critical of the war. Now the northern Whigs began to divide into right and left wings over the issue of what strategy to follow on the war. The conservatives, called the Cotton Whigs, were suffering a crisis in their Puritan conscience. Their desire for peace conflicted with their desire for profits. The economic interest in more slave-grown cotton for their textile mills made the lords of the loom sensitive to offending their brother Whigs in the South. The Cotton Whigs would rather not call the Mexican War the result of a slaveholders' plot. They preferred the softer ground of objecting to the war as aggressive and unconstitutional. It was the line Daniel Webster, their leading spokesman in Congress, took, when he accused Polk of usurping the Constitutional powers of Congress. "What is the value of this Constitutional provision," he asked, "if the President of his own authority may make such military movements as must bring on war?"

The radicals, called the Conscience Whigs, were not content with Constitutional arguments. They gave new vigor and broader organization to the protest of the abolitionists. Such younger men as Charles Francis Adams, Horace Mann, John G. Palfrey, Charles Sumner, and Henry Wilson launched a new party daily, the *Boston Whig*, to make sure the Conscience wing had as loud a public voice as the Cotton wing.

The *Boston Whig* made plain how it saw slavery in the political picture:

Either the present tide, which is carrying all of our institutions, excepting the forms, into a vortex of which slavery is the moving power, must be stayed by the peo-

ple of the free States, or, if left to its course, it will bring on, in no very long time, a sudden and total dissolution of the Union. . . . We feel tolerably confident it may be avoided; but it can only be done by one way. That way is the total abolition of slavery—the complete eradication of the fatal influence it is exercising over the policy of the general government.

That grim prospect of a "total dissolution of the Union" was exactly what the Cotton Whigs feared too. Both wings of the party wanted to prevent it—the Cotton Whigs by burying all talk of slavery as an issue in this war, and the Conscience Whigs by shouting their belief that the extension of slavery was the very heart of Polk's purpose in prosecuting the war.

Whatever their party or other differences, the people who opposed the war would find a rallying point for their resistance in something that happened in the summer of 1846.

9

DAVID, THE GIANT-KILLER

The August night was unbearably hot. Summer was never a time to be confined to Washington. But in this summer of 1846 the 29th Congress had business to take care of—Polk's business of running a war. The House of Representatives was in session that evening to debate the President's request for $2 million to "facilitate negotiations" with Mexico.

A stout, blond man with ruddy face was on his feet, asking for the floor. David Wilmot, Pennsylvania Democrat popular with his southern colleagues, had an amendment to offer to the appropriations bill. The few words he put it in would throw Congress and the nation into wild excitement. He waited a moment for silence, then read out his brief rider:

PROVIDED, *That, as an express and fundamental condition to the acquisition of any territory from the Republic of Mexico by the United States, by virtue of any treaty which may be negotiated between them, and to the use by the Executive of the moneys herein appropriated, neither slavery nor involuntary servitude shall*

ever exist in any part of said territory, except for crime,
whereof the party shall first be duly convicted.

The next morning he rose to find the Wilmot Proviso
had made him famous. "God raised up a Daniel of old
to slay the giant of Gath," roared a New Yorker. "So
hath David Wilmot with the sling of freedom and the
smooth stone of truth, struck the giant Slavery between
the eyes. He reels; let us push him over."

The key words of the proviso, "neither slavery nor
involuntary servitude," were taken deliberately from
Jefferson, who had used them in the Northwest Ordi-
nance of 1787 to keep slavery out of the territory north
of the Ohio River. Around Wilmot's measure a coalition gathered: antislavery Whigs, abolitionists, and anti-
Polk Democrats. The issue now, said Wilmot, "is not
whether slavery shall exist unmolested where it now is,
but whether it shall be carried to new and distant regions, now free. . . . I ask not that slavery be abolished.
I demand that this government preserve the integrity of
free territory against the aggressions of slavery."

His challenge raised the tension to a still higher pitch.
No longer was this a case of mere protest. Now Polk's
opposition was trying to tie the hands of the administration. Several times the proviso passed the House, but
in the Senate southern Whigs joined southern Democrats, and northerners with southern principles, to reject
it. The rider was never adopted. But its political po-
tency was enormous. It was a statement of principle,
a platform to unite antislavery elements. And as such it
worked. The debate that raged around it revealed the
realignment of political forces in the nation. Whigs and

David Wilmot.

Democrats began to think of themselves as northerners or southerners. One after another ten northern legislatures endorsed the proviso, while southerners condemned it. The South knew the northern position would check the spread of slavery and reduce the political strength of the slave states. And they were angered by the speeches denouncing slavery as immoral. Especially when Wilmot showed he was not prompted by any sympathy for the black man. "I plead the cause of the rights of white freemen," he said. By banning slavery from any territory to be gained from Mexico he meant to preserve the place for "the sons of toil, of my own race and own color."

Calhoun took the lead in defending the South against its enemies' "foul slanders." He warned:

Sir, the day that the balance between the two sections of the country—the slave-holding and the non-slave-holding states—is destroyed, is a day that will not be far removed from political revolution, anarchy, civil war, and widespread disaster. . . . But if this policy should be carried out, woe, woe, I say, to this Union!

Calhoun insisted the territories belonged to all Americans. Not only did Congress have no right to discriminate against the private property (read *slaves*) of Southerners, he said; it had the Constitutional obligation to protect slave property in those territories. And he offered a series of resolutions to that effect. This only intensified northern suspicion that the South wanted to grab pieces of Mexico to spread and strengthen slavery.

As verbal volleys over the war were exchanged in the

halls of Congress, Zachary Taylor was preparing to carry the offensive from Camargo to Monterrey, a city of some 15,000 people located at a key point in northern Mexico. In mid-August the general loaded the supplies he had collected and began his advance. Along the way his troops picked up Mexican broadsides calling the war anti-Christian and urging the Americans to desert.

It was just at this moment that the often discredited Santa Anna returned from exile in Cuba. In the decade since his disgrace at the hands of the Texans he had been in and out of power more than once. In 1843 he had been tumbled from Number One position once and for all, everyone thought, and had fled to Havana. But his hopes rose again as he watched the war clouds gather after the annexation of Texas. Surely some sort of deal would restore him to power. He let Washington know he was prepared to negotiate a quick end to the war if he could be put in the right spot. Polk was interested. But first Santa Anna had to get back into Mexico. His moment came when Gomez Farias whipped up a revolt in May 1846. By arrangement with Polk, Santa Anna slipped through the American naval blockade and landed in Vera Cruz. "The Americans," wrote Justo Sierra, "with the most cunning Machiavellianism, had let him through, as if they were tossing an incendiary bomb into the enemy's camp. . . . Alas, this soldier who was not good enough to be a general was going to be Commander in Chief."

Meanwhile, Taylor was nearing the outskirts of Monterrey, leading an army of 6,000 men. The city was considered impregnable: it was protected by a river and mountains on three sides, and strong forts completed the defenses. Here the Mexicans under General Ampudia had concentrated 7,000 troops. After reconnoitering, Taylor decided on a two-pronged assault. He would move directly on the town while General William J. Worth would make a flanking attack to take the Saltillo Road. This would cut off the enemy's main supply route as well as his only path for retreat.

Bombardment began on September 20, and heavy fighting in mist and rain followed day after day. The Mexicans were gradually forced back to the heart of their city. On September 23 Worth and Taylor converged from opposite sides, their men fighting their way through the streets house by house. Surrounded at last, Ampudia feared American shells might blow up his powder magazines. On the morning of September 24 he offered to surrender the town. Taylor, wanting to avoid further bloodshed and running dangerously low on ammunition and food, granted him generous terms. Ampudia was allowed to withdraw his troops with their arms while the Americans promised not to push deeper into Mexico for another eight weeks. The next day the Mexican army left. The Americans ran up the Stars and Stripes and began their occupation to the booming of 28 guns. Taking the town had cost the Americans 800 killed and wounded.

The news swelled Taylor's reputation among the folks back home. His political star rose higher on the crest of the celebrations. The army's prestige, too, grew with each victory. But again professional soldiers criticized Taylor's generalship. Benjamin Franklin Cheatham, a twenty-six-year-old captain of Tennessee volunteers, thought little of the way "Old Rough and Ready" handled

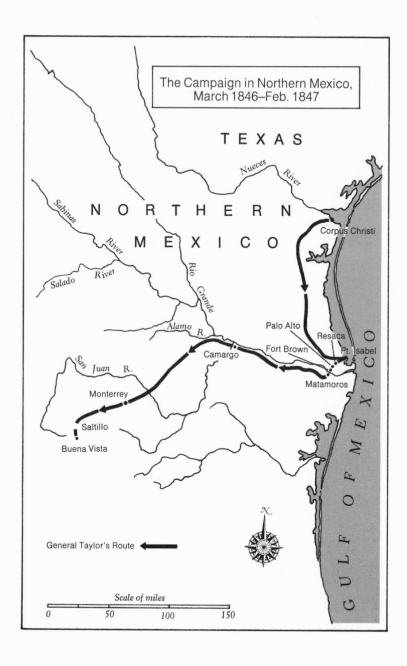

The Campaign in Northern Mexico,
March 1846–Feb. 1847

TEXAS

Nueces River

NORTHERN

MEXICO

Corpus Christi

Sabinas River

Salado River

Rio Grande

Alamo R.

Palo Alto

Resaca

Fort Brown

Pt. Isabel

San Juan R.

Camargo

Monterrey

Matamoros

Saltillo

Buena Vista

General Taylor's Route

N

GULF OF MEXICO

Scale of miles

0   50   100   150

the attack on Monterrey. In letters home to his sisters he wrote:

I consider that old Taylor committed one of the greatest blunders that ever a General was guilty of in coming here to attack one of the strongest fortified towns in Mexico, with nothing in the world but small artillery for open field fighting. . . . We took into the field three hundred and forty men, and had killed and wounded one hundred and four. So you see that we had killed and wounded near one third of our force, which is a thing almost unheard of. The Mexicans say that we are the first people that they ever saw run up into the cannon's mouth, they wanted to know where we came from, and what kind of people we were. . . .

I must here say, that I consider that our division of the army was badly managed, that we were rushed headlong into the fight, even our Generals did not know where we were going and what our situation was until we found ourselves under a deadly cross fire of cannon balls, shells, grape and musketry, from three different forts, without any chance of extricating ourselves except by charging at the mouth of the cannon, the forts in our front.

Democratic politicians too, from the President on down, joined in the attacks on Taylor. The frequency with which the winner's name was being proposed as the Whig choice for President made them nervous. Polk didn't mind letting the public know that "In agreeing to this armistice Genl. Taylor violated his express orders and I regret that I cannot approve his course." And in his diary Polk wrote: "I am now satisfied that he is . . . without resources and wholly unqualified for the command he holds."

Lieutenant Meade put another interpretation on why Taylor had granted so generous an armistice:

That we had the Mexicans completely in our power, and could have slaughtered the greater part of them before they could have made their escape, was well known to the whole army. It was no military necessity that induced General Taylor to grant such liberal terms, but a higher and nobler motive. First, to grant an opportunity to the two Governments to negotiate for peace, knowing, as he did, that should he destroy the Mexican army, the Government would never listen to overtures of peace under the disgrace. Secondly, to stop the unnecessary effusion of blood, not only of soldiers, but of old and infirm women and children, whom necessity kept in the city, and who were crowded with the troops in the small space they had retired to, and were surrounded by our troops, from whom every shot told. Thirdly, as a tribute of respect to the gallantry of the Mexicans, who had defended their place as long as it was in their power.

With Taylor settled in at Monterrey for the eight-week truce, we can look at another sector of Polk's campaign plan. One of the President's goals was to capture New Mexico and California. On May 13 he had ordered Missouri's governor to raise eight companies of dragoons and two of light artillery to take New Mexico. Little resistance was expected. New Mexico's governor, Manuel Armíjo, was known for bluster not bravery, and

*Storming the Bishop's palace at Monterrey,
Mexico; painted by Samuel Chamberlain.*

the loyalty of people given little but heavy taxes was questionable.

In command of his Army of the West, Polk placed Colonel Stephen W. Kearny, a veteran of the War of 1812 and of thirty years of service on the western frontier. Some 1,700 volunteers were easily enlisted and briefly trained at Fort Leavenworth. In June they began their long march on Santa Fe. They crossed prairie and plains, suffering from heat, thirst, and short rations until they reached Bent's Fort and the Arkansas River in mid-July. There word came that Armíjo had assembled 2,300 men to defend Santa Fe and that another army was gathering at Taos. It looked like a hot fight after all.

While Kearny's tired troops rested, the colonel laid plans for a bloodless conquest. He sent word ahead through captured New Mexican spies that those who did not resist American occupation would be protected. Then he pledged civil and religious freedom for all who would lay down their arms. And finally he delegated James Magoffin, a Santa Fe trader who spoke Spanish and knew Armíjo well, to travel ahead under a flag of truce in order to attempt negotiations with the governor.

Early in August, Kearny's army left Bent's Fort and headed for Santa Fe. Two weeks later an emissary from Armíjo met them to threaten resistance if they continued their invasion. Kearny ignored the warning and marched ahead, occupying village after village along the way. On August 18 he reached Santa Fe to find Armíjo had fled the town.

Why? We know Magoffin had met with Armíjo and in long talks had argued it would be better for the governor to "submit to fate." President Polk, the American said, wanted "only to give peace and prosperity to the inhabitants." Kearny was on his way with strong troops. Futile to resist them, he said to a man he knew would rather not fight. Later, Magoffin would put in an expense chit for $50,000 to reimburse him for "secret services rendered during the war." Armíjo was known for his venality as much as for his cowardice. It is not unlikely, then, that he was bribed to fade away without a fight.

So, only six weeks after his campaign started, Kearny, now promoted to general, had control of New Mexico without firing a shot. He raised the American flag and proclaimed to the citizens that he had taken possession of New Mexico in the name of the United States. He promised protection of persons and property. Kearny worked out a code of laws and a territorial constitution, and named Charles Bent the civil governor. Thinking the situation secure, General Kearny split his troops into three groups. He ordered Colonel Sterling Price to stay in Santa Fe to control the province. He sent Colonel Alexander W. Doniphan south to subdue some Indians and to capture Chihuahua. And he himself, carrying out Polk's orders, started with three hundred dragoons for California, to take a hand in its conquest.

The men assigned to occupation duty grumbled at their dull task and wondered how long they would be sweating out this war. They eased their boredom with drinking and brawling. The civilians soon were sick of the "bullying and overbearing demeanor" of their new rulers. Their resentment became focused on Governor Bent.

That December a plot to kill Americans came to light. Colonel Price tightened controls which worsened the civilians' discontent. In January rebellion broke out at Taos, where Bent and his staff were visiting. The sheriff was killed and then the governor. As Bent's body was dragged through the streets, mobs murdered all the Americans they could find. In the end, fifteen lay dead and the survivors were racing for Santa Fe with the terrible news.

Colonel Price took five companies of troops and headed for Taos. He routed two large bands of rebels on the way. Reaching Taos he stormed the town. After he had killed 150 people, the resistance was broken.

On his march to California, General Kearny ran into Kit Carson bound for Washington with official news that the territory of California had been freed of Mexican control and was now in the possession of the Americans.

How had this phase of Polk's strategy been accomplished? Recall that back in October 1845 Polk had sent word to Thomas O. Larkin, his confidential agent in California, that if the territory could be separated from Mexico by "the free and spontaneous wish" of her people, it would be embraced by the United States. What he meant was that Larkin should seize any chance to promote a Texas-style revolution that would end in the annexation of California. At the same time Polk prepared other means of acquiring California. He told Commodore J. D. Sloat, head of the Pacific Squadron,

A California lancer, 1847.

that if war should break out with Mexico he was to capture San Francisco and other major points. When the shooting began on the Rio Grande, Sloat got orders to take Monterey and to blockade whatever ports he thought necessary.

Polk's other plan was based upon a "scientific" expedition he asked army Captain John Charles Frémont to lead in California. The Georgian-born officer, now thirty-three, had carried out several surveying projects when the Army Engineers commissioned him. His marriage to the daughter of Senator Thomas Hart Benton of Missouri boosted him into leadership of several expeditions to the Rocky Mountains. His reports, ghosted by his wife, Jessie, earned him fame as the "Great Pathfinder."

With Kit Carson as guide, the Frémont party reached California late in 1845. The sight of sixty frontiersmen, all armed, prowling about the countryside, made the Mexicans suspicious. Ordered out of the province, Frémont challenged the Mexicans to try and throw him out. But Larkin intervened and Frémont moved his men up to the Oregon line where they stood by for the next stage in California's troubles.

California was in poor shape to stand off any aggressive moves by outsiders. The white population of the province numbered only 5,000; about 700 of these were Americans, with no stake in Mexican control of California. California had recently seen a struggle for power between Mexican leaders which threatened to bring on civil war. Polk, apprised of the turmoil, moved to take advantage. He sent marine lieutenant Archibald H. Gillespie to Larkin and Frémont with oral messages whose meaning no one yet knows. In any case, Frémont's response was to march at once into California. Some historians think Polk sent him word to foment a revolution by American settlers against Mexican authority. Others suggest Frémont had decided on his own to cast himself in the role of a Sam Houston with a mission to conquer California.

A group of American settlers staged the "Bear Flag Revolt," and when Frémont came on the scene, they declared the "independence" of California. A few days later word arrived that the United States was officially at war with Mexico. The Bear Flag was promptly hauled down and the Stars and Stripes run up in its place. Frémont left for Monterey to join forces with the U.S. Navy in completing the conquest of California.

As soon as the navy had gotten news of General Taylor's battles on the Rio Grande it had begun carrying out its standing orders. It captured Monterey and proclaimed California to be a part of the United States. Shortly afterward, it seized San Francisco, Sonoma, and Sutter's Fort.

With a common enemy to worry about, the Mexicans buried their differences and prepared for a stand at Los Angeles. But there was to be no fight; the garrison fled into Mexico as the Americans approached. On August 17, 1846 (while Taylor was at Camargo), the U.S. proclaimed the annexation of California. Like New Mexico, California was taken almost without a gun being fired. But again, as in New Mexico, "peace and harmony" did not last long. The Mexicans revolted at the end of September.

After a few engagements with the Americans, what

was left of the enemy forces capitulated to Frémont (who had done no fighting) and signed the Treaty of Cahuenga on January 13, 1847.

Eight months after his war message to Congress, Polk had won two major prizes—New Mexico and California. But these conquests were only on the fringes of the conflict. The war would not be won this far from the heart of Mexico.

10

BUENA VISTA

You couldn't miss General Winfield Scott, whether he was with his troops or, as now, in the fall of 1846, plumped in his chair at the War Department. The Virginian towered six feet four and one-quarter inches. (Let's not forget that quarter-inch; he wouldn't.) It was infuriating—worse, embarrassing—to be general in chief of the United States Army, and not be allowed to get near the battlefield. Polk had refused to put him in command of the troops that were fighting against the Mexicans.

The reason was simple, and political. It had nothing to do with Scott's qualifications as a soldier. Now sixty, Scott had been in the army for almost forty years. He had made a fine record in the War of 1812. Wounded several times, he had shown the brilliance and bravery that win medals and promote a captain to brevet major general. The war over, he went abroad twice to study the military tactics of European armies, and wrote military manuals which became gospel in the U.S. Army. Then came service against the Indians in that long series of wars of expulsion and extinction—first the Black Hawk, then the Seminole, and finally as leader of the army which "escorted" sixteen thousand Cherokees on the tragic Trail of Tears from their homeland in the southeast to Indian territory on the far side of the Mississippi. With such a record of achievement Scott had risen to the top post in the army. Or nominally the top, for the President, as commander in chief, made the important decisions.

While the rank and file called Zachary Taylor "Old Rough and Ready," the vain and pompous Scott they called "Old Fuss and Feathers." In the nicknames you can see the difference between the two generals. Unlike Taylor, Scott had the polish that came from a proper family background. He was at home in Washington's high society. His uniforms were many and gorgeous and so were his speeches. He "always wore all the uniform prescribed or allowed by law," said Ulysses S. Grant, "and was not averse to speaking of himself often in the third person."

But mannerisms to the side, Scott knew warfare and had argued from the outbreak of the conflict that the way to beat Mexico was to drive straight for her heart —Mexico City. It would never be done by agonizing marches from the northern border down across the great desert. Do it the way Hernando Cortez smashed the Aztecs, he said. Land at Vera Cruz and fight your way into Mexico City.

It was sound advice—only it came from a Whig with presidential ambitions. Twice Scott had been talked of for his party's nomination, the last time as recently as 1844. Polk wasn't taking any chances in 1846, halfway to the next presidential election. He sent not Scott but "Old Rough and Ready" to do the fighting. True, Taylor was a Whig, too, but not nearly as prominent as Scott.

By the time November came around Polk was having second thoughts. While Taylor's northern campaign had been successful, no final victory had been won. The Mexican troops were still in the field, with Taylor even guaranteeing them two undisturbed months to rest and regroup. Taylor's victories, however limited, had made him the man of the hour. Too many were thinking he was God's chosen instrument to carry out America's Manifest Destiny. If he could be removed from center stage . . .

Still another thread in Polk's thought was the necessity to do something about the shrinking enthusiasm for the war. If Scott's proposal were adopted, and a quick thrust at central Mexico succeeded, it would bring the war to a happy conclusion and end the dissension at home.

Polk's political fears darkened when he saw the results of the November elections. His Democrats lost the House of Representatives and the Whigs made marked gains everywhere in the country but in the Deep South, where they at least held their own. Inevitably the Whigs' electoral success would heat up their attacks on Polk, his party, and his war. The President confessed to his diary that he was feeling himself more and more in the minority. Even the bill for recruiting the ten more regiments he felt were vital to carrying on the war was running into grave trouble in the Congress.

Forced onto the defensive, Polk once more tried to convince the country that the war was all Mexico's fault. Mexicans had crossed *our* boundary, the Rio

Grande, to shed American blood on American soil, he said in his annual message to Congress of December 8, 1846, giving nearly ten thousand words to this question of "war guilt." Whigs who accused him, Polk, of being the aggressor were "giving aid and comfort to the enemy." By which he meant they were traitors.

So reckless a charge made the Whigs furious. This "foul imputation," they replied, was intended to intimidate them. They would not be silenced. But how far would they go in their opposition to the war? Most Whigs continued to vote men and supplies for the fighting while still attacking the war as evil and unconstitutional. In self-justification they argued that Congress could not desert an army sent into the battle. The war, right or wrong, had been voted by Congress, and now the troops must be supported.

That defense was not swallowed by Joshua Giddings. On December 15 he tried to demolish such reasoning by drawing a parallel between this war and the American Revolution. Remember what the great British Whigs did in that era, he said. Charles Fox, Lord Chatham, Edmund Burke, and others denounced the British attack upon the American colonies as an unjust and aggressive war. They would not vote supplies for it and demanded the withdrawal of British armies from their war of conquest. We, too, said Giddings, we American Whigs have a moral obligation to use similar means to force Polk to get out of Mexico.

A Cotton Whig, Congressman Winthrop, abhorred such radical proposals. He answered that British precedent did not apply because the defeat of a supply measure would bring down a British administration and put a

From a recent Photograph by Brady.

Winfield Scott
Lieut Genl. &c &c.

General Winfield Scott.

new one in office. Here in the United States no vote of Congress can change our administration, he said. It would simply paralyze it until its term of office ended.

The Conscience Whigs did not accept that argument. Columbus Delano of Ohio got the floor to reply. Whether in England or America, he said, the object of withholding supplies is to stop the administration in its career of mischief and lawlessness. In both countries the withholding of supplies compels the government to change its policies. The end to be obtained is the same. The fact that our President is elected for a term of years does not make him independent of Congress during that time. He then went to the heart of the Constitutional issue:

I am unwilling to sanction, even by silence, a doctrine which puts this country, for a period of four years, so entirely, absolutely, at the mercy of one man—a doctrine which throws at once the reins of government upon the neck of executive power, and gives the steed full license to trample upon the liberties and lives of the people. The framers of the Constitution never looked for such an interpretation of it. They expressly reserved to Congress the right to declare war; they knew that money was necessary to wage war; and they supposed that as long as the power to grant and withhold supplies remained with the Congress, the President, by a judicious exercise of this power, would be restrained from prosecuting any war longer than shall be necessary and proper.

Two days later Luther Severance, a Whig from Maine, followed up Delano's argument with a simple point-by-point brief.

I will here enumerate fourteen reasons why I am still opposed to prosecuting the war, and why I cannot vote further appropriations to carry it on. These reasons are:

1. Because the war was wrongfully and unjustly commenced by the President, while Congress was in session, without asking its consent.

2. Because it is a war of conquest, and was commenced, and is now continued, with that design.

3. Because war did not exist by the act of Mexico, and did not exist legally until Congress recognized it in May last.

4. Because there is no other way in which I can, by my vote, manifest my opposition to the continuance of the war.

5. Because, in refusing men and money to prosecute the war in a foreign country, I do not endanger the safety of a single individual, or a single interest, in my own country.

6. Because the war is a prodigal squandering of human life and national treasure, without any benefit to the country or to mankind.

7. Because a war between the two largest republics in the world is not calculated to spread the principles of civil liberty and elective government.

8. Because an acquisition of territory, for the purpose of establishing slavery where it has once been abolished, would be turning backward in the march of civilization, and be a national calamity, even were the acquisition bloodless, honestly obtained, and without cost.

9. Because, even if the territory acquired be made free, aggressive war is not an approved mode of extending the "area of freedom," or of obtaining respect for republican principles.

10. Because I regard as utterly absurd any attempt to force a people into our Union against their consent.

11. Because, if we had their consent, we should be better off without them.

12. Because the money foolishly spent in this war by the two countries would have built a railroad and a line of telegraph to Oregon, and a ship canal across the isthmus.

13. Because all war, but that which is strictly defensive, ought, in this age of the Christian world, to be regarded as criminal and barbarous.

14. Because the triumphs of peace are far more glorious and more enduring than those of the sword.

Ten months after he had voted aye on Polk's first war bill, Senator Thomas Corwin of Ohio electrified the country with one of the most scathing indictments of a President ever heard on the floor of Congress. In a three-hour speech he charged Polk was "something of a King . . . who does very much as he pleases," a "haughty, imperious" man guilty of "a bold falsification of history," of "usurpation of authority," of "all-grasping avarice," of behaving like a "robber chief," of carrying on a "desolating" war on the pretext that the rapidly growing American population would soon need more room. "If I were a Mexican," said Corwin, "I would tell you, 'Have you not room in your own country to bury your dead men?

If you come into mine, we will greet you with bloody hands, and welcome you to hospitable graves.' "

In some ears that speech sounded like gross treason. Ohio Democrats demanded Corwin be put in prison for the duration of the war. To the antislavery Whigs, however, Corwin looked like the man who could stop the nomination of Zack Taylor. Their press hailed the senator as the "people's choice."

Corwin and other antiwar Whigs had voted supplies and men whenever Polk asked for them. An unknown young man from Illinois, upon entering Congress in 1847, did the same thing. Abraham Lincoln declaimed against Polk's war, and went on voting supplies for it. Outraged by Polk's distortions of the truth, he defied the President to name the spot where American blood had been shed upon American soil. His "spot resolutions" won him brief fame but lost him support from the voters back home. They made this his first and last term in Congress, and the prairie lawyer sank back into obscurity—for a time.

With the 1848 election on the horizon, the Whigs cast about for a candidate who could beat the Democrats. They found him in Zack Taylor, hero of the war they denounced. To nip that in the bud, Polk made two moves. He recommended that Congress create a new rank in the Army, "lieutenant general." The purpose, he said, was to make possible a unified command of both the regulars and the volunteers now in service. His real aim, however, soon ferreted out by the Whigs, was to put the Whig generals, especially Taylor, in the shade of a Democrat. The man he had in mind for the supreme command was Senator Thomas Hart Benton.

While this proposal came to nothing in Congress, Polk's other plan, requiring no one else's approval, went through. In his diary for November 14, 1846, the President revealed how he prepared the way:

The Cabinet fully discussed the conduct of General Taylor and were agreed that he was unfit for the chief command, that he had not mind enough for the station, that he was a bitter political partisan, and had no sympathies with the administration.

The next step was to adopt Scott's plan to drive for Mexico City by way of Vera Cruz, and to appoint "Old Fuss and Feathers" to the supreme command. It was politically risky. Polk was taking the spotlight away from one Whig general and shining it on another. But he had little choice if he meant to win the war.

To hold Taylor down, Polk instructed him to confine his operations to the Monterrey line. Taylor's great displeasure was increased when Scott notified him that he would need 9,000 of Taylor's experienced troops for the new expedition. Taylor began to feel that conspirators in high places were plotting his downfall. "I am constrained to believe that I no longer possess the confidence of the administration," he said. "Why not relieve me altogether?" The troops Scott wanted were sent to join the expeditionary force at Tampico. But Taylor defied the orders to stay on the defensive. In February 1847 he quit Monterrey and marched the raw troops left him to Saltillo, 70 miles to the southwest. He took the town without firing a shot.

General Wool and his staff at Saltillo.

Meanwhile, Santa Anna had made his carefully staged return to Mexico City. José Fernando Ramírez watched the general's entry from his balcony windows:

Santa Anna rode in the Government's state coach, an open carriage. He sat there on the main seat, sunk down among the cushions, with the big banner of the federal constitution fluttering from its staff at his right. The size of the banner with its attached streamers and tricolored ribbons made it almost impossible for him to sit down. Farias rode on the front seat, facing him and the banner. Both men were silent and seemed more like victims than conquerors. Santa Anna was dressed in quite a democratic fashion: a long traveling coat, white trousers and no crosses or medals on his breast. So terrible was the impression all this produced on me that when the coach got to a place opposite my balcony windows, I drew back involuntarily, being seized with such a violent headache that I was no good the rest of the day. I do not know what sort of terrible, foreboding thing I could possibly have observed in that scene.

Santa Anna found Mexico's treasury empty. A war could not be carried on without money. While he mustered a fresh army at San Luis Potosi, he set Gomez Farias and the Congress to producing funds. The only rich treasury belonged to the Church. So a bill was passed empowering the government to mortgage a portion of Church property for 15 million pesos. By merciless levies on the regions surrounding San Luis Potosi, Santa Anna built up his army to 20,000 men.

What shape was Mexico in now, nine months after the start of the war? As Justo Sierra saw it:

The situation of the country was this: our ports were blockaded, most of the states paralyzed, the northern ones lost; Yucatan, seceding again, declared itself neutral so as not to fall into the Americans' power; the deficit soared to seven to eight millions; the press clamored against the government; the people of the capital formed battalions of militia, some to support the dominant reformists, others, of the middle class, to prevent any sacrilege against the clergy, who, less from patriotism, perhaps, than from fear, parted, sobbing bitterly, with tiny fractions of their fortunes.

As for Santa Anna, angered by a steady drumfire from the press berating him for doing nothing, he decided to engage the American army in battle. But which one? Scott's army assembling at Tampico, or Taylor's in the north? He made up his mind when his scouts intercepted a letter from Scott to Taylor which not only told Santa Anna about the planned expedition to Vera Cruz but gave him the reduced number of troops left under Taylor's command. The Mexican general decided to march northward and destroy the weakened Taylor first. And then he would take care of the defense of Vera Cruz.

The decision meant he had to cross a terrible desert in winter with no tents and meager supplies, and with troops he had not yet had time to give even basic training. He marched anyway, said Sierra, "across that interminable stretch of desolation, dust, and thirst, toward Saltillo and by the time he made contact with the enemy he was already beaten. He had lost four thousand men in his battle with the desert."

When he reached the vicinity of the Buena Vista hacienda where Taylor had taken up his position with 5,000 men, only one-tenth of them regulars, Santa Anna sent word to Taylor that he had a four-to-one superiority and threatened him with catastrophe unless he surrendered unconditionally within an hour. The confident Taylor refused.

On the afternoon of February 22 fighting began, pausing at nightfall without any conclusive results. The next morning Santa Anna made a powerful attack on the American left flank and drove the Americans into confused retreat. Disaster was imminent when Taylor hurried up with reinforcements. They halted the Mexican charge and forced the troops back. In the afternoon Santa Anna began another strong attack on the left, seeking to gain control of the Saltillo road on the American's rear. Bloody hand-to-hand fighting took place through a heavy rainstorm, and the Mexicans slowly fell back. Taylor's men regained the lost ground and saved their rear. There was another American assault later that afternoon which cost Taylor dearly, followed by a final Mexican thrust against the center of the American line. When Taylor's artillery began to mow down the Mexicans, Santa Anna called his men back. The fighting could be called a draw. Both sides had severe losses, the Americans about 700 killed and wounded, the Mexicans perhaps 1,800.

That night Santa Anna weighed his choices. He could risk sending his battered troops into another battle in the morning, or he could retreat now with his army still intact and display the guns and flags he had captured early in the battle of Buena Vista. In the morning the worn-out Americans discovered the Mexicans had chosen

The Battle of Buena Vista, from an on-the-spot sketch by Taylor's aide-de-camp.

to pull out under darkness. Although he had been assailed for failing to capitalize on his victory at Monterrey, Taylor would not ask his exhausted men to chase the Mexicans. "The great loss on both sides," he wrote his brother, "had deprived me of everything like pleasure."

To one of the West Pointers at Buena Vista, the behavior of the volunteer units seemed abominable. Captain Braxton Bragg of North Carolina, who led a battery, thought Taylor's dispatches on the battle were "generously full so far as good conduct went, but rather silent on the subject of volunteers running." Bragg told the truth about the volunteers as he saw it, in a letter to his soldier-friend William T. Sherman:

The great Baltimore battalion which boasted so much of taking Monterrey fled in a body very early in the action and never got into the fight. From five companies but nine men remained on the field at night. . . . The extolled Texans in every instance were not sustained and, urged on by regular troops, have retreated—frequently in shameful confusion. . . .

At the Battle of Buena Vista we were whipped, and in retreat when Genl. Taylor arrived on the ground. Three regt. were in full retreat—but few of these ever returned to the field, and when the day closed we could not have mustered 2,500 men. It is a fact, asserted by our Medical Officer, that the wounded in the hospitals were trampled to death by refugees endeavoring to hide and pass for sick or wounded. And yet, that was a volunteer victory!! If any action in the whole war, Cump, proved the inefficiency of Vols. that is the one.

The retreat proved a disaster for the Mexicans com-

Illustration from the sheet music of "Buena Vista," 1847.

parable to the fate of Napoleon's army after Moscow. The hungry, demoralized troops left their wounded behind and threw away their weapons as they stumbled south. Their wagons broke down, and with the roads clogged many conscripts disappeared into the hills. Remembering that they were "carried off by the levy and educated by the rod," as Sierra put it, they ran away. By the time San Luis Potosi was reached, Santa Anna's 20,000-man Army of Liberation had dwindled to 11,000.

Buena Vista ended the campaign in northern Mexico. For the rest of the war the American troops would simply hold the line they had established there. Taylor's defense of Buena Vista won him no honors from the President. Polk thought it was a battle that need never have been fought—and one that certainly rated Taylor none of the honors the press and public again heaped upon him. In Polk's eyes the general was still an old fool whose reputation had been made for him by his men. The glory of winning the war would not be Taylor's. But he would return home later that year reaching for the Presidency that politicians were already dangling before him.

Buena Vista

Near Buena Vista's mountain chain,
Hurrah! Hurrah! Hurrah!
Brave Taylor met his foes again,
Hurrah! Hurrah! Hurrah!
Though thousands to our tens appear,
Our boys have hearts that know no fear,
Hurrah! Hurrah! Hurrah!
Hurrah! Hurrah! Hurrah!

That day heard Santa Anna boast,
Hurrah! Hurrah! Hurrah!

Ere night he'd vanquish all our host,
Hurrah! Hurrah! Hurrah!
But then the braggart did not know
That Taylor never yields to foe!
Hurrah, hurrah *etc.*

Kentucky by brave Maryland led,
Hurrah! Hurrah! Hurrah!
Seeks vengeance for her gallant dead,
Hurrah! Hurrah! Hurrah!
And while for Vaughan, McKee, and Clay
The tear-drop flows, they win the day!
Hurrah, hurrah *etc.*

There's Hardin brings up Illinois,
Hurrah! Hurrah! Hurrah!
With Bissel's line of gallant boys!
Hurrah! Hurrah! Hurrah!
And Indiana, led by Lane,
All bravely struggle on the plain!
Hurrah, hurrah *etc.*

O'Brien, Sherman, Washington,
Hurrah! Hurrah, Hurrah!
Their batteries pour the foe upon;
Hurrah! Hurrah! Hurrah!
While Captain Bragg, at "Zack's" command
"More grape" bestows on every hand!
Hurrah, hurrah *etc.*

Young Arkansas, whose gallant yell,
Hurrah! Hurrah! Hurrah!
Amidst the din of battle fell,
Hurrah! Hurrah! Hurrah!
Still claims brave Pike her sons to lead,
Soon to avenge the bloody deed!
Hurrah, hurrah *etc.*

No page in history e'er can show,
Hurrah! Hurrah! Hurrah!
So bright a victory o'er a foe,
Hurrah! Hurrah! Hurrah!
As we this day did proudly gain
On Buena Vista's bloody plain!
Hurrah, hurrah *etc.*

11

I ABOMINATE THIS WAR

Just as the battle of Buena Vista was being fought, a regiment in Mexico City mutinied. The revolt of the *Polkos*, the people called it, because the rebels were upper-class dandies who spent more time on the ballroom floor than on the drill ground. The mutiny occurred when the regiment was about to leave the capital for the defense of Vera Cruz, and seemed to be gotten up by the clergy as a way of protesting the government's attempt to force a loan out of them.

The government, already distraught, was paralyzed for three weeks while all sorts of rumors flew about. News arrived that Santa Anna had been defeated at Buena Vista by a narrow margin; to many outraged patriots the defeat was interpreted as a deliberate betrayal rather than the familiar blunder. Santa Anna had not been beaten by the enemy; he had beaten himself. Whispers of Santa Anna's peculiar relations with Polk gained plausibility when the *New York Herald* printed a report that the general had made a secret treaty with the United States, promising to hand over parts of Mexico gradually, in return for an American guarantee that he would be lodged in the Presidency for ten years.

When Santa Anna returned from Buena Vista, both the clergy and the rebel regiment welcomed him as a victor. He promptly complied with their demands and repealed the assessment on Church property. The disgusted anticlericals charged that the nation was nothing but a backward province of the Church: how could it ever meet the test of war? The scandal caused so heavy a loss in moral authority that the hierarchy retreated and handed Santa Anna more money than the disposal of Church property would have brought.

What the Mexicans had to face now was Scott's projected landing at Vera Cruz. In the latter part of February 1847, the American general massed an invasion armada and 10,000 troops at the Lobos Islands, about seven miles off the Mexican coast, below Tampico. (He had been promised 20,000 men, but his army never exceeded 14,000 and sometimes dropped as low as 9,000.) Here he got his forces ready and made plans for the invision. It would be the largest amphibious attack that American troops had yet attempted.

Like Taylor, Scott was not a West Pointer. Unlike Taylor, he knew that there were gaps in his military experience and welcomed men with superior training. Around him in this campaign he had a brilliant group of young officers, West Point men with the technical knowledge he lacked. Such officers as U. S. Grant, Robert E. Lee, George G. Meade, George B. McClellan, and P. G. T. Beauregard—who would hold top commands in the Civil War—were among his informal staff. It was the first war in American history which gave West Point a chance to show the quality of its graduates. The regiment, brigade, and division commanders were almost all

"Old Fuss and Feathers."

men of no formal training. Most of them were amateurs. Of the general officers, only Worth and Twiggs were professionals. The West Pointers on the lower echeleons were therefore all the more valued by Scott. Young though they were, he listened to them. The engineers especially he used for close staff work, asking careful reconnaissance of terrain and enemy positions from them before making his tactical and sometimes even strategic decisions.

As the Americans prepared their invasion, some of the officers thought about why they were here, and what this war was for. Lieutenant Meade confided to his wife:

You know my sentiments; opposed, at first, to this war, brought on by our injustice to a neighbor and un-called-for aggression, she in her stupidity and folly, giving our rulers plausible excuses for their conduct; but when once in it, I should and have desired to see it conducted in a vigorous manner, and brought to a speedy conclusion by its being carried on with energy well directed. But such has not been the case, nor will it ever be so, as long as generals are made in the counting-houses and soldiers on farms.

That feeling about the war was shared by a veteran officer, Lieutenant Colonel Ethan Allen Hitchcock, who had been commandant of cadets at West Point and was now Scott's acting inspector general. In a letter he wrote February 27 to the abolitionist preacher Theodore Parker, Hitchcock said:

I coincide with your views of this abominable war. Humble as I am, I wish not to fall a victim to this war without entering my protest against it as unjust on our part and needlessly and wickedly brought about. I am here, not from choice, but because, being in this army, it is my duty to obey the constituted authorities. As an individual I condemn, I abominate this war: as a member of the govennment I must go with it until our authorities are brought back to a sense of justice.

On March 2 the fleet sailed from its anchorage and made rendezvous four days later at a point 12 miles south of Vera Cruz. After two days of reconnoitering, Scott felt ready. Vera Cruz had few defenses on the landward side. Protection seaward was provided by a stout wall flanked by two forts. And on a reef in the bay sat a fortress defended by 2,500 troops with batteries. General Mora had been promised men and money to strengthen the city's defenses, but the Mexican government was in such chaos no aid ever came. As Scott approached, all but 3,000 of the civilians fled to the hills.

Scott decided against a frontal assault because its human cost would be too great. His choice was to land men on a beach a few miles south of Vera Cruz, thus bypassing the fortress on the reef and the massive wall toward the sea.

On March 9 the landing began. The assault troops moved from their transports into surf boats. Private George Ballentine, an English volunteer, described the landing:

The scene was certainly exciting and imposing: the military bands of different regiments stationed on the decks of the steamers, transports, and men-of-war, played the national airs of "Yankee Doodle," "Hail Columbia," and "The Star-Spangled Banner."

At a signal from the vessel having General Scott on board, the boats simultaneously gave way for shore, leaving a considerable space vacant in front of our men-of-war, who were anchored next the shore, and had their guns double-shotted, ready to open upon the enemy, should they make their apearance. The gun-boats, meanwhile, continued to tack backwards and forwards for the same purpose. Under the circumstances, it was plain that the Mexicans could not prevent us from landing, but, by waiting until the first party were fairly on the sands, they might assault them with a very superior force, when our gun-boats and men-of-war would be prevented from firing, by the fear of injuring our own men. This was the event we almost expected to witness, and, as the boats neared the shore, we watched the result with intense anxiety, expecting each moment to see a body of Mexican cavalry charge over the sand-hills. But no such event occurred . . . not a single Mexican was to be seen. The American flag was immediately planted amidst loud and prolonged cheers, which were enthusiastically echoed by the troops on board. All idea of there being any fighting for that day, at least, was now at an end, piquets were thrown out, and sentries posted on the most advantageous points of the heights to guard against a surprise; the men began to make themselves at home; we could observe fires were kindled, and camp kettles swinging on them, in less than an hour after they had landed, and before evening the beach had all the appearance of a camp.

U.S. troops landing at Vera Cruz.

The Mexican failure to resist the landing was a great gift to the Americans. During the next week Scott built up his supplies on the beach and prepared a siege of the city. By blocking it from the rear, he would prevent the Mexicans from escaping or from getting help. On March 22 he demanded a surrender, and when refused, began to bombard the city. His guns fired so fast at night that the shells appeared to be a constant stream in the sky. The Mexican batteries fired back, but their gunnery was poor.

Scott's siege guns moved closer and closer to the city (helped by the naval batteries offshore), breaching the walls gradually and doing great damage inside them. In a week the city's morale crumbled and the Mexicans surrendered. Scott occupied Vera Cruz on March 29, at a cost of 19 Americans killed and 63 wounded. The American flag floated over the city as the Mexican troops marched out, paroled on their word not to fight again. Private Ballentine was jubilant, but when he walked into the city to see the effects of the bombardment, his delight in the "easy victory" was damped down:

The whole of the southwest side of the city, which, lying nearest our batteries, was most exposed to the storm of destructive missiles, was a scene of desolation calculated to make the most strenuous advocates of physical force pause and reflect. For my own part, while ready to admit the whole weight and force of such powerful arguments, I felt strongly inclined to doubt the justice or propriety of having recourse to them. Whole streets were crumbled to ruins, and they told us the killed and wounded inhabitants amounted to between five and six

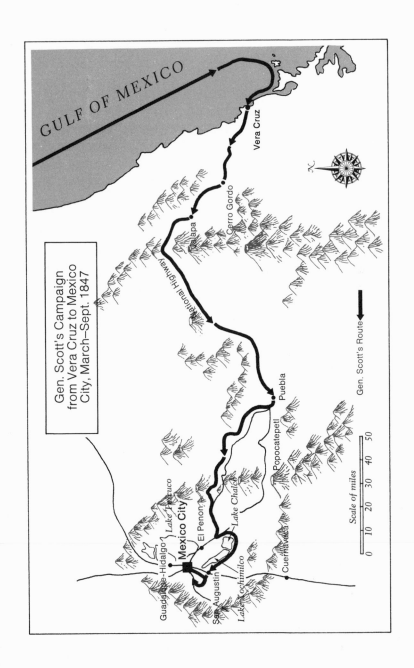

Gen. Scott's Campaign from Vera Cruz to Mexico City, March–Sept. 1847

GULF OF MEXICO

Vera Cruz

Cerro Gordo

Jalapa

National Highway

Puebla

Popocatepetl

Cuernavaca

Lake Texcuco

El Penon

Lake Chalco

Guadalupe-Hidalgo

Mexico City

San Augustin

Lake Xochimilco

Gen. Scott's Route

Scale of miles

0   10   20   30   40   50

hundred, while the soldiers who had been employed at their batteries during the whole time of the bombardment had as many more; the entire killed and wounded being over a thousand.

With Vera Cruz in his hands, Scott now had a base from which he could begin the march overland to the enemy's capital. Santa Anna, who had taken over the presidency meantime, was furious when he learned that Vera Cruz had surrendered. He put the presidency temporarily in the hands of General Anaya, and set out to stop the American advance on the capital. He wanted to make his stand beyond Jalapa, his home ground. He chose the canyon of Cerro Gordo, bringing up 12,000 troops for its defense.

Scott's line of march into the interior was along the National Highway, the route Cortez had taken. It begins with some 55 miles of lowland, then rises like a rugged staircase through steep mountain canyons to the high plateau on which Mexico City sits.

On April 8 a division commanded by General Twiggs started up the highway, followed the next day by General Patterson's troops. Scott demanded speed, hoping to get his army to Jalapa, high about the coastal lowlands, before the deadly *vomito*, or yellow fever, attacked.

When the Americans reached a village below the pass at Cerro Gordo, they met Mexican fire and halted. Santa Anna had placed his defense line across the National Highway, anchoring it on a river at one end and on two hills at the other end, El Telégrafo and La Atalaya. The first peak was protected by one hundred men with four pieces of artillery.

The Mexican general was sure the Americans could move only along the highway, and had concentrated his fire there. His reserves he stationed at the main camp in the rear of his line. In two days, when his engineers had completed their reconnaissance, Scott decided that a frontal assault would be suicidal. Instead, he would make a deceptive move against the Mexican right wing, while sending his strongest force to the flank and rear of the left wing. He picked troops familiar with mountain territory to cut paths up the steep slopes on the bypass route, lugging with them some heavy howitzers.

Early on the morning of April 17 Scott ordered Twiggs to begin the battle. Twiggs seized La Atalaya on the Mexicans' extreme left, placing artillery on it. He then tried to ascend El Telégrafo but was repulsed. The next morning Scott opened up with artillery as General Gideon J. Pillow made a diversionary assault on the Mexican right. But that commander, an amateur appointed by his former law partner, President Polk, botched it badly, suffering heavy losses. When the howitzers secretly placed on La Atalaya the previous night opened fire, the Mexicans were astonished; they had not believed that the big guns could be gotten into place by any route except the highway. Twiggs' men crossed the ravine between the two hills and charged up El Telégrafo. Against heavy resistance they succeeded in driving the Mexicans from their position. Meanwhile, the American force which had sneaked around the Mexican left flank launched an attack on the enemy's rear. Their unexpected appearance threw the Mexicans into great confusion. They fled in disorder down the hill and along the road to Jalapa, Santa Anna and his staff among them. By ten in the morning the battle of Cerro Gordo was over.

Jacob Oswandel, a canal boatman from Pennsylvania who had volunteered at the age of twenty-one, wandered over the battlefield, and recorded what he saw:

The Mexican wounded were strewn all over the field; some with their arms and legs off, some shot almost in two and still gasping, some with their entrails hanging out, screaming with pain and agony, begging for a gota de aquas (a drop of water); we gave them water out of our canteens, and eased them of their misery all we could. It would puzzle the best artist in the world to paint the picture in its true light, or as we saw it. We saw the paroled Mexicans hunting up their dead and wounded comrades; to some of the dead they gave a decent burial, and the wounded they took proper care of; others of the dead they gathered in heaps and burned. Thus it is plainly to be seen that the twenty-four pounder played havoc among the enemy.

We also saw the body of the gallant Mexican Gen. Vasquazes. . . . and, I regret to state, that some of our moral soldiers, who, after the battle of yesterday were sent out to bring in our dead and wounded soldiers, not only rifled his pockets, but took off his boots and all his mountings. In fact nearly all the dead Mexicans had their pockets turned inside out, to see whether they had anything in them. This thieving operation on the dead seems to be the custom. . . .

Mexican casualties at Cerro Gordo amounted to more than 1,000 men. In addition, they lost 3,000 troops in prisoners taken, about 4,000 small arms, and 40 cannon.

The Americans suffered 64 dead and 353 wounded.

The next day the Americans occupied Jalapa. While Scott remained there to gather provisions and make further plans, General Worth's troops went on to take Perote and then Puebla. The last town fell with only a slight push. The clergy, the gentry, and the local commandant had decided not to resist the enemy. They had heard Scott abolished taxes wherever he went, and let the church alone. And his troops gave business a good boost. But Santa Anna suddenly appeared with 2,000 cavalry and attacked Worth's army as it came up. The demoralized Mexicans caved in quickly and fled with their general toward Mexico City. On May 15 Puebla was securely in American hands.

Scott's most pressing problem now was how to persuade his volunteers to remain in service. Their enlistments were for a twelve-month period, and that time was nearly up for many who had fought from Monterrey to Cerro Gordo. Oswandel said the volunteers had not been paid one cent since joining up. When they finally got some money in May, it was only $17.50, two months' pay.

General Scott tried to entice them with bounties as well as appeals to their patriotism, but to no avail. They had fulfilled their obligation, they felt; now let others share the burden equally. With their service up in only six weeks, Scott decided to let them go at once. When Jacob Oswandel heard the "great shouting and cheering" that went up as the "good news" reached the lucky regiments, he cried, "Oh! didn't I wish myself to be one of them!" He visited the men on May 6, their last morning in service:

This morning is a glorious one to the discharged volunteers. We went to their camp and gave them a hearty shake of the hand and bid them good luck and safe return to their homes. Telling us that they deeply regretted to leave us almost in the midst of the enemy's country, that they would like to be with us and march on to the capital of Mexico, but the United States Government had fooled and bamboozled them so often, that they have no faith in it; and seeing no sign of the government prosecuting the war with vigor, and seeing no reinforcements arriving, they began to think that the Government is in no hurry to crush this war. The contractors have not made enough money, and the quartermasters have not robbed the poor soldiers enough of their rations. . . .

About 8 o'clock, A.M., the reveille was called. . . . When they started off, they gave us remaining troops three hearty cheers, and bade good-bye to "Camp Misery."

The short-term enlistments cost Scott about one-third of his effectives—seven regiments and two companies of volunteers. He was left with 7,000 men when he moved his headquarters to Puebla at the end of May.

In the towns the Americans occupied, Mexicans told Private Ballentine that they believed Santa Anna was the cause of their defeat at Cerro Gordo. "He left precipitately an hour before the storming . . . by his example so discouraging the officers and men that they soon after broke and ran, believing the battle lost."

12

A SUMMER IN PUEBLA

Puebla in the summer of 1847 was a sorry place. The morale of the American troops fell to a dangerous low. "Their conduct towards the poor inhabitants has been horrible," wrote Captain E. Kirby Smith to his wife, "and their coming is dreaded like death in every village of Mexico." The men suffered from the heat; they felt the hatred of a hostile citizenry; they drilled senselessly for too many hours; and dysentery, moaned Private Ballentine, afflicted almost all:

The sick list and the hospitals were full to overcrowding, and one-half of those doing duty, wasted with diarrhea, looked like skeletons or mummies; the hardships and privations of the previous part of the campaign, telling more or less severely on nearly àll, and one could not walk far through the streets of Puebla without hearing the mournful strains of the soldiers' funeral procession. At Perote too, where a large number of sick had been left, the castle having been converted into a depot, the sick died at the average rate of twelve-a-day for a series of months. These were interred without any military formalities, or even the usual burial services, being wrapped in the blankets in which they died, they were carted out and thrown into pits dug for the purpose daily outside the garrison.

Writing home during this grim summer lull in the fighting, Captain Smith let his wife see how much his feelings had changed since the war began:

How differently I feel now with regard to the war from what I did then! Then vague visions of glory and a speedy peace floated through my brain. Now I have learned in common with many other poor fellows that it is not he who patiently does his duty, or who in the hour of danger is in the front of the battle, who gains the laurel or the more vulgar reward of government patronage. It is too frequently the sycophant who flatters the foibles of his commanding officer, he who has political family influence, or whom some accident makes conspicuous, who reaps all the benefits of the exposure and labors of others. The long list of brevets, most outrageously unjust as they are, many of them double, is a register of evidence to the facts that success is a lottery and that government rewards are by no means dependent on merit. How tired and sick I am of a war to which I can see no probable termination! How readily would I exchange my profession for an honest, mechanical employment, were it possible to do so! How instantly would I resign if I saw any certainty of supporting my family in tolerable comfort or even decency in civil life!

As the news of yet another victory, at Cerro Gordo, reached New York, the city was turning out for a "Grand Celebration and Illumination" in honor of the American troops. The dazzling display was described in the *New York Herald*:

The City presented a grand and gorgeous spectacle from sunrise to late at night. At sunrise the booming of American cannon from the Battery resounded from the Narrows to the Palisades. The repeated echoes had not died away when, as if by the hand of an invisible sorcerer, ten thousand flags and banners of bunting, of brilliant hue and large dimensions, were thrown to the breeze and floated gaily and joyfully over the City Hall, Custom House and other buildings. At noon a salute of one hundred guns was fired from the Battery, Washington Square, Tompkins Square, and Harlem.

Two o'clock being the time appointed for the procession to leave the Battery—an hour before that time found Broadway crowded with pedestrians of all ages, conditions, sizes, and colors. The elite and the unwashed million rushed, by common consent, towards the Battery . . . and cheered with the greatest enthusiasm as company after company of our citizen soldiers wheeled into line or threaded the gravel walks to their appointed places.

The scene on the Battery was indeed imposing. . . . Dashing officers in bright uniforms mounted upon proud chargers pranced about the ground—adjutants flew from post to post—companies marched, counter marched, and then stood sternly by their arms. . . . Those hardy sons of the cleaver as cavalry, the sharp shooting riflemen, with an infantry force hardly surpassed in discipline, would be a hard nut for any foe to crack.

At sunset the city began to pour its inhabitants into

the streets to witness the magnificent illuminations and fireworks. The surrounding country sent its thousands over the different ferries to join in the same pleasure; the streets were never so densely crowded, nay packed, with human beings.

Such joy, celebrated by civilians a thousand miles from the battlefields, was never felt by the men in uniform. "I now despair of leaving this country for years," wrote Captain Smith to his wife on July 7. "Bitter, most bitter, is my conviction that such is to be my fate, and I can but wish that none were united to me and compelled to be miserable on my account. . . . Alas, the chance is I shall never see you again!"

Two months later he was killed in action.

It was a trying time for Scott's army at Puebla. He gathered in troops stationed in nearby towns but still had not enough strength to advance on the capital. All summer long he sweated out reinforcements. In between training periods his men explored the town. Captain Anderson complained to his wife of the rapid rise in prices. A fork or a spoon cost fifty cents now, and an iron dipper a dollar and a half. His wife wanted to know how the ladies dressed in Mexico, but so far, he said, they have refused to show themselves to us "barbarians." He could describe the dress of the common people, however:

The men wear jackets, pantaloons of buckskin, blue cloth or velvet, fitting tight around the waist and open on the outer seam, ornamented with buttons, or lace, embroidery, etc., the inside lined, and shewing under them another pair of pants; this under-garment is in-

Mexican people.

variably white. Over the shoulders, they wear the universal blanket.

Their hats have very broad brims and almost invariably ornaments at the side, a band or two of silver lace where we wear the hat band, and sometimes lace around the circumference of the brim. On horseback, their legs are protected by a large piece of skin or leather, attached in front of the stirrup leather, which covers the leg perfectly. The foot is doubly protected, first by the huge wooden stirrup, secondly by a thick flap of leather which is fastened to the upper part of the stirrup.

The common women wear the chemise (I suppose) and over it fastened around the waist some petticoats, the outer one entirely of some fancy colored material. Over their heads, breasts, and shoulders, you again see the blankets, or ribosa which is worn by all who can afford it. These are placed on the crown of the head (sometimes fastened to the hair by a pin) crossed so as to meet about the chin.

The artillery officer told his wife too of Puebla's marketplace and what you could find in it:

The common sponge-cake sold in the streets is generally excellent; then you find figs, dates and various kinds of rinds, exceedingly well preserved; again you find other sweetmeats, of which milk is a component part. Their candied fruit is very good. I hope that on our return I may find transportation for a box or two of these articles for you.

The toys and dulces are exhibited for sale under the arcades of the large houses separated by streets from the Plaza where the market is held. The market is to strangers a great curiosity, being held in a large open square.

Mexican street scene.

Along the outer side of the square, you find Mexican crockery, plates, dishes, cups, bowls, water jars, baskets (willow). . . .

The first row inside is corn, next to this you find onions, large and white as snow, tomatoes, generally of the wild kind, green and about an inch in diameter, and some coarse kind of greens, parsley, etc.

Next are some women who have their charcoal furnaces at work cooking and selling various Mexican stews, etc.

On the next row among the onions, cabbages, tomatoes, large and small (I have not seen any of the beautiful golden tomatoes here), radishes (very large and good), turnips, squashes, peas, carrots. . . .

In the next row, you find fruits, baskets of pears, mostly green, indifferent peaches, apples and cherries, Mamaias in abundance, small apricots, sapotes both green and blue (neither good for anything) alligator pear, and, for a rarity, here is a woman who has some mushrooms.

Under that awning, you find oranges, limes, muskmelons, watermelons (six cents a slice), goat's cheese, eggs, chocolate makers, coarse wooden spoons, etc., . . . you find cooking utensils, earthen and iron, and near by, the chickens, turkeys, and pigeons. Those piles of white chalky-looking substance are lime, used in cooking, etc. On Thursday, the great market day, you find piles of beans of all colors and sizes. Flowers are also seen frequently in Market—pinks appear to be favorites. The cocoanut is very fine, but I think the plantain the best fruit I have seen. I have also omitted the fruit of the cactus, two kinds, green and purple. Peppers abound always. These are in little piles on matting—the women sitting by them in a way peculiarly Mexican, on their legs

Mexican marketplace.

doubled under them; all sit in that way.

Looking beneath this surface, Private Ballentine speculated on the role of the church in bringing Mexico to its present condition:

There are said to be more than a hundred domes and spires in this city, which has a population of 80,000. It abounds in convents, and each of these distributes daily an allowance of provisions at the convent door, without money and without price, or even the formality of a ticket from a member of the mendicity society; a discriminating charity being no part of the policy of the Church of Rome, one of whose deliberate aims seems to be the fostering of ignorance and poverty. To endeavor to unfetter agricultural, manufacturing, and commercial industry, and to have the accursed law of peonage abolished, so that the people might gradually emerge from this miserable serfdom to a more elevated and self-dependent state, would scarcely suit the views of that Church. . . . Every stranger who visits Mexico, and does not wilfully shut his eyes to the fact, must perceive the culpability of the clergy in causing and perpetuating the present condition of affairs. They seem to have cared about nothing but the endowment of churches, ornamenting of shrines, and all the childish mummery of their pageantry. Under the present system of religious intolerance which prevails in Mexico, it cannot be expected that the country will become progressive or prosperous.

To Colonel Hitchcock, distinguished for brilliance of literary style as well as intellect, General Scott gave a special assignment that summer. He was to draft an appeal to the Mexican people, putting it in simple language all could understand. It was to summarize the history of the war and the issues on which it was being fought. Its true purpose, said the colonel in his memoirs, was "to prove the Americans wholly right in their war of invasion."

In spite of the fact that Scott's message was directly opposed to his own personal beliefs, Hitchcock carried out orders with his customary skill. Ten thousand copies of what he wrote were printed on broadsides in both English and Spanish and distributed to the Mexicans. Like the congressmen who spoke up against the war but voted men and money to carry it on, Hitchcock apparently could rationalize his action and avoid a conflict with his conscience. The last words in his manifesto read: "We are here for no earthly purpose except the hope of obtaining peace."

The Mexicans living in occupied territory did not let the invaders rest easy. Guerrilla bands sprang up to harass the Americans. Jacob Oswandel was one of the volunteers routed out of camp to hunt the guerrillas. Of course he had small enthusiasm for such a task:

These guerrillas are composed of men, mounted on spirited mustangs, well-equipped with rifles, pistols, carbines, daggers, lances and lassoes. They generally have good and brave officers, but the rest of them are the most wretched and desperate ruffians in the country, such as assassins and pardoned felons, pardoned on the terms of joining the guerrillas. They are mostly divided into different bands, and each party is accompanied by a Catholic priest, there being no other religion allowed in this country. This priest's duty is to first swear each one upon the cross to watch every chance, if they can see their way clear, to pursue the enemy (us Americans) to their death, their motto is, "No quarters to the Yankees."

They generally put themselves on or by the road-side to attack provision and specie trains and murder the soldiers who may, from fatigue, lag behind our army; and sometimes they even cut our men's throat, heart and tongue out, hanging them on a limb of a tree right over their bodies; they also stop and murder our scouts, messengers, etc. They are promised one-half of all of the provisions and specie they can plunder from our army.

This is the character of the guerrillas, which, no doubt, you have read a good deal of. They carry a flag with cross-bones and skull, with the words, "We give no quarters." They have now succeeded in cutting off our communication between here and Vera Cruz, but it is rumored that Gen. Frank Pierce has left Vera Cruz with fifteen hundred men, who will, if they come across them, strike terror to these national licensed highway robbers. Then our communication will again be open.

During the skirmish with the infernal guerrillas, we have suffered more frightfully than at the battle of Cerro Gordo with the regular Mexican army. In fact, we would sooner face ten of the regular Mexican army than one of these outlawed guerrillas.

13

TWIN BATTLES

Early in August Scott decided the time had come to move on Mexico City. His army had swelled to 14,000 men over these ten weeks at Puebla (although 3,000 of them were too sick to perform their duties), and he had built up the supplies needed for the advance.

The last reinforcements to arrive were 2,500 men of the 9th New England Regiment, commanded by Franklin Pierce. A devoted New Hampshire Democrat, Pierce had declined the cabinet post of Attorney General offered him by Polk in favor of enlisting as a private in the volunteers. In six months he had rocketed to the rank of Brigadier General. (Later, in 1852, he would defeat Winfield Scott for the Presidency.)

In Mexico City, as the people awaited Scott's next move, the situation was "truly desperate," said José Fernando Ramírez. In a letter to a friend outside the capital he confided:

Everything, absolutely everything, is lost, and judging by the way things are going it is doubtful whether we can save our independence, the last refuge and symbol of our honor. The animosity and indolence of the politi-

cal parties that have been quarreling over the possession of power have left us only two ways of escape: either conquest or a peace settlement that will always be a shameful one, because we do not have the strength to reject any peace terms that may be offered us.

There were many who wanted peace, he said, especially among the remnants of the broken army, but while no one "is brave enough to propose peace," many were "brave enough to let themselves be conquered without a struggle." None of the factions could agree on how to defend the city. The federal district was placed under martial law and the states were asked to send troops and money, which they failed to deliver. There had been too many broken promises for the Mexicans to have any faith in leaders who delivered nothing. When Santa Anna returned to the capital after his flight from Puebla, he jailed his opposition and made himself president-dictator. But no one—neither the people nor the state regimes—rallied to his banner. Not even the clergy supported him.

Ramírez wrote that in this terrible hour he was one of those "who, fearing everything from war, see nothing attractive in peace." A peace settlement, he believed, would bring "disaster and upheaval" and the country would be "destroyed by inflamed factions without honor, patriotism, or culture." He was so gloomy over the prospects of resistance that he thought Scott could occupy Mexico City without firing a shot.

There were other intellectuals like Ramírez who had little or no faith in the defense of their land. Justo Sierra said they argued that it was "impossible to vanquish an army that can be reinforced endlessly from the north and from the east. And what if we do lose lands that never belonged to us except in name: Texas, California? Perhaps that would be an advantage; a reduction in size might make for cohesion, concentration, strength."

Sierra says many of the people, however, had only "hatred and contempt" for the invaders who were "a race incompatible in custom, language, and religion." They felt they must beat the Yankees, but "they failed to recognize what was admirable in that valiant and level-headed handful of intruders who, taking advantage of the superiority of their armament and their cohesion and of the inefficiency of Mexican generals and the damaging dissensions of civil war, had penetrated to the heart of the country, sweeping all before them."

Santa Anna pushed furiously, using cannons cast from church bells, confiscating muskets from citizens and buying them from foreigners, making gunpowder, forging bayonets. Desperate for money, he let Scott know that a treaty might be arranged for the proper consideration: ten thousand dollars down and one million when peace was made. Scott was tempted. He discussed it with his officers. Some opposed paying a bribe for peace because it was immoral and would embarrass and humiliate the folks back home. Scott decided it would not injure anyone's integrity because "the overture, if corrupt, came from parties already corrupted." We had already bribed Indians and Barbary pirates, and a million-dollar peace would be cheaper than a protracted war. The end justified the means, in short. Scott took the ten thousand out of a secret service fund. After pocketing it, Santa Anna decided he could keep the Americans out of the capital and cut them off from retreat to the coast. Financial negotiations were broken off.

By midsummer the Mexican commander had concentrated a force of 5,000 regulars and 8,000 militia in the capital, together with some 12,000 civilians he had conscripted. These 25,000 troops he organized into three armies. His plan was to defend the city on its perimeter by militia stationed at fortifications that had been swiftly thrown up. His regulars he would hold in the center for dispatch to any threatened point. A second army under Juan Alvarez was directed to swing behind Scott so as to cut him off when he retreated, and the third army was ordered to Guadalupe Hidalgo, a suburb north of the capital.

As the Americans approached, Santa Anna issued a proclamation to the people. "Blinded by pride," he said, "the enemy have set out for the capital. For this, Mexicans, I congratulate myself and you."

The natural defenses of the capital were excellent. The city was surrounded by marshes (once large lakes) and to penetrate it the enemy would have to cross by one or more of the causeways linking Mexico City to the countryside. Santa Anna's outer defenses had been put up at all the key points of entry. He fortified the main northern approach at Guadalupe Hidalgo and the southern approach at Mexicalcingo. Between them, on El Penon, the hill overlooking the main road from the east, he prepared his strongest defensive point.

Scott started out from Puebla on August 7, 1847, with about 11,000 men. He organized his troops into four divisions led by Worth, Twiggs, Pillow, and Quitman. The cavalry he put under Harney, while he himself took control of the engineers, the dragoons, the howitzer and

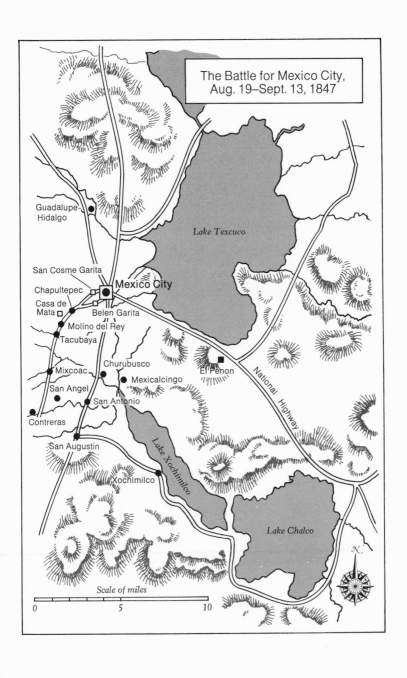

The Battle for Mexico City,
Aug. 19–Sept. 13, 1847

Guadalupe-
Hidalgo

Lake Texcuco

San Cosme Garita
Chapultepec
Casa de
Mata
Belen Garita
Molino del Rey
Tacubaya
Mixcoac
Churubusco
San Angel
Mexicalcingo
El Penon
San Antonio
Contreras
San Augustin

Mexico City

National Highway

Lake Xochimilco

Xochimilco

Lake Chalco

N.

Scale of miles

0   5   10

rocket battery, and the siege train. Twiggs went out front, the others following, keeping half a day's march between them so that they could reinforce one another if attacked on the route. Then came the train of a thousand supply wagons, stretching out for three miles. Trailing them was the unofficial army of editors, reporters, printers, gamblers, teamsters, merchants, and women.

After several days the troops reached a high point where they could view the far-famed valley of Mexico, captured only once before by Hernando Cortez. Private Ballentine struggled to find words for his first sight of the plateau and the capital which crowned it:

At an elevation of about 3,000 feet, the spectator sees, as if spread at his feet, like a map, the whole of the valley of Mexico, its circumference, at the base of the mountains which form the sides of the mighty basin, being 120 miles, and at the crest of the mountains 200 miles. The whole of the plain, from the height on which the spectator stands, is distinctly taken in at one view, and the most minute details are distinctly defined and delineated, owing to the remarkable transparency and purity of the atmosphere.

The towers and spires of the city of Mexico, 25 miles distant, are distinctly seen peering out from the foliage and trees; almost the only part of the valley where trees are to be seen, by the by, is that round the city. The remainder of the valley presents the uniform appearance of a large green plain, dotted with white churches, spires, and haciendas, and containing several large sheets of water, the remains of the lakes which are said to have once nearly covered the whole valley. Several small insulated mountains may also be distinctly discerned, the only large objects that rise on the surface of the vast unbroken green plain. The mountains of Popocatepetl and Itzaccihuatl, its brother giant, rise about 20 miles to the left, and tower to a height of 7,000 feet higher than where the spectator is standing, though owing to the bright atmosphere and the sun shining on the snow, it seems only two or three miles distant. The whole of this beautiful valley is hemmed in by a circle of stupendous, rugged and dark mountains, the rough but sublime setting of nature is one of her most inimitable pictures, and forming a most perfect combination of the sublime and beautiful.

Seen from that elevation, the valley of Mexico is a most glorious and magnificent sight, but " 'tis distance lends enchantment to the view," and we descend into it, its beauties vanish. The lakes become marshes, the fields are not cultivated, the villages are mud, and the inhabitants wretched-looking Indian peons, in rags and squalid misery.

The army camped near Chalco, the village on the lake of that name, and waited for Scott's engineers to carry out their reconnaissance. They reported only three possible approaches to the city—straight through on the road from Vera Cruz; a right turn that would bring them to the city from the north; or a left turn southward by the Mexicalcingo route. There were serious problems with all of them. After weighing his choices, Scott decided to attack by Mexicalcingo.

Almost immediately, however, he changed his orders. Robert E. Lee and P. G. T. Beauregard, two of his engineer officers, had just found a fourth possibility—a route lying south of the lakes of Chalco and Xochimilco, skirting the base of the mountains to reach San Augustin, a village ten miles south of the capital on the road to Acapulco. Santa Anna had left this route, an area of wasteland and cold lava flow, unguarded. He believed no army could travel over it. He was wrong. On August 17 the Americans took San Augustin after only some light skirmishing.

The decision to go the San Augustin route was a major blow to Santa Anna's plan of defense. By this flanking maneuver Scott had made the Mexicans' strong fortifications useless. The effect was double: the news crippled the Mexican army's morale and gave a great lift to the combative spirit of the Americans.

Now Santa Anna had to improvise rapidly. He moved guns from El Penon to a point just north of San Augustin. He also called in General Valencia's army which had been stationed north of the city.

But instead of heading straight for Mexico City via San Antonio, Scott again outflanked the Mexican defenses. He left some troops to make a demonstration there, while sending the rest of the army westward to capture the San Angel road.

Santa Anna guessed this possibility and shifted General Valencia's forces south of the same area, where they set up a defense near Contreras. About noon on August 19 the Mexican guns opened fire on Twiggs' and Pillow's columns advancing through the lava field on Contreras. The crashing of small arms mingled with the relentless roar of artillery. The fighting lasted for six hours. The Americans moved ahead slowly because they had to build a road for their advance while under steady fire.

Disaster threatened just before dark, when Santa Anna himself moved in from the north with troops that menaced the Americans by placing them between two Mexican forces. As Santa Anna started a cannonade, a violent storm came up; he had to withdraw in the dark to San Angel, ordering Valencia to abandon his position as well. The general refused to obey "for very good reasons," as Ramírez reported.

One of these reasons was the fact that the enemy had an open road to enable him to occupy Tacubaya, the key to Mexico City. In spite of this the order was repeated, with the additional command that if Valencia had to abandon all our supply trains and munitions to effect this move he was to do so. He again refused to obey, and thus the disagreement reached the point where Valencia informed Santa Anna that his conduct was that of a traitor and that he would not require his help. The next morning Valencia was surrounded by the enemy army that had profited by the darkness of night, and no one came to help him.

At three o'clock on the morning of August 20 the Americans began to slip around Valencia's rear. To fool him they left a token force in their camp, with fires burning. They also sent troops to attack on the Mexican's front. When dawn came the Mexicans opened artillery fire on the Americans facing them. Suddenly the Mexicans were hit from the rear. Captain Smith, taking part in the battle, described what happened at Contreras and immediately after at Churubusco, about five miles farther up the road:

The Battle of Churubusco.

Early on the morning of the twentieth, the attack was made and the works carried at the point of the bayonet, scarcely a gun being fired. We took fifteen hundred prisoners and twenty-two pieces of artillery among which were the guns captured by Santa Anna at Buena Vista. As soon as the result was known to General Worth, the Second Brigade of his division with our battalion were put in motion to endeavor to turn the position at San Antonio. For two hours we ran over the rocks moving by a flank, the enemy in a heavy column marching parallel to us and almost in gun shot, until the head of the Fifth Infantry pierced their line and the fight began at a quarter before twelve. It will be entirely impossible for me to give any lucid description of this terrible battle. It extended over a large space and I could see but little of it, being too hotly engaged to notice much beyond the sphere of my own duties. Our battalion when the firing began must have been near a half mile to the rear. The "double quick" was sounded and the whole advanced at a run. We soon reached the road and turned in hot pursuit.

Along the road to this point I had seen no wounded or dead American, though on either hand and in the road were many dead Mexicans. We had advanced on the road less than a mile when we were ordered into the fields to assault the right of the enemy's position—I am speaking of our battalion.

At this time the battle was fiercely contested on our left and front. . . . Immediately in front of us, at perhaps five hundred yards, the roll of the Mexican fire exceeded anything I have ever heard. We had not from our battalion as yet fired a gun, but now rapidly advance, all apparently eager to bring the contest to a hand to hand combat in which we knew our superiority.

We could not tell what was before us—whether the enemy were in regular forts, behind breastworks, or delivering their fire from the cover afforded by the hedges and ditches which bordered the road and fields—all was hidden by the tall corn.

We soon came out of it into a crossroad near some small houses, where we were exposed to a dreadful cross fire, which could scarcely be resisted. Many had fallen and the battalion was much scattered and broken. My men were just formed and I had ordered the charge which I was about to lead, when the dreadful cry came from the left and rear that we were repulsed. A rush of men and officers in a panic followed, running over and again breaking my little command. I shouted that we were not repulsed—to charge—and the day would be ours.

Up to this time we were not aware that the other divisions of the army were engaged, but we now learned that Twiggs and others were pressing them on the left and had been fighting them an hour or more. Before this we had discovered we were under the fire of two forts. Now as the whole army shouted and rushed to the assault, the enemy gave way, retreating as best they could to Mexico [City]. They were pursued by all, hundreds being shot down in the retreat, our Dragoons charging after them to the guns at the gate of the city, where they were stayed by a tremendous discharge from the battery covering the entrance.

The battle over, Captain Smith, tired and sore as he

was, went back to collect the dead and dying of his battalion:

The field presented an awful spectacle—the dead and the wounded were thickly sprinkled over the ground— the mangled bodies of the artillery horses and mules actually blocking up the road and filling the ditches. In the battalion there was in the aggregate fifty killed and wounded out of about two hundred and twenty engaged; in our entire division, three hundred and thirty-six; in the whole army, one thousand fifty-two. I thank God for my escape which I now think wonderful.

The loss of the enemy must be immense. Their officers say, in killed, missing, and captured, they have lost over five thousand. They acknowledge that they had twenty, some say thirty thousand, in the fight. It was a wonderful victory and undoubtedly the greatest battle our country has ever fought, and I hope will bring peace. . . .

In those twin victories at Contreras and Churubusco, Scott almost shattered the Mexican army. The weapons and ammunition he seized trebled the strength of his siege train and field batteries. The American losses were 131 killed, 865 wounded, and 40 missing. The Mexicans —in addition to the dead, wounded, and captured estimated by Captain Smith—lost thousands through desertion. There was nothing new in that. The United States, too, in all its wars has lost soldiers through desertion. But in the Mexican War the American deserters did something extraordinary, something that had never been done before in the history of the United States Army.

14

TRAITORS—OR MARTYRS

The American soldiers who deserted in the Mexican War did not just quit fighting and run away. They switched to the enemy's army and fought against their former comrades. It makes a curious chapter in history. Private Ballentine, who fought at Churubusco, left us this account of what happened there:

Among the prisoners taken at this engagement were seventy deserters from the American army. They were tried by a general court martial shortly after the battle, and being found guilty of the crime of desertion were sentenced to be hung, which sentence was carried into execution in presence of a portion of the troops shortly before we entered the city. I sincerely pitied these poor fellows, many of whom I had reason to believe had been driven to the foolish step they had taken by harsh and cruel usage, operating on a sensitive and excitable temperament.

The barbarous treatment which soldiers sometimes received from ignorant and brutal officers, and non-commissioned officers, on that campaign, were I to relate it in minute detail, would seem almost incredible. I have frequently seen foolish young officers violently strike and assault soldiers on the most slight provocation; while to tie them up by the wrist, as high as their hands would reach, with a gag in their mouths, was a common punishment for trivial offenses.

A variant of this punishment was called "bucking and gagging." The soldier was placed on his back on the ground. His outstretched arms and legs were tied to stakes, and his mouth gagged. So common was it that the troops composed a song called "Bucking and Gagging" to the old English tune of "Derry Down." Note the reference to desertion caused by such treatment.

Ballentine went on to say:

In fact, such a bad state of feeling seemed to exist between men and officers throughout the service that I was not surprised that it should lead to numerous desertions. If our men had not known how utterly wretched was the condition of soldiers in the Mexican service, deserting to which was literally jumping out of the frying-pan into the fire, I believe that numerous as these desertions were they would have been infinitely more so. These deserters were considered a principal cause of the obstinate resistance which our troops met at Churubusco, two or three attempts of the Mexicans to hoist a white flag have been frustrated by some of them, who killed the Mexicans attempting to display it. The large number of officers killed in the affair was also ascribed to them, as for the gratification of their revenge they aimed at no other objects during the engagement.

Military historians agree with Ballentine that Churu-

Bucking and Gagging

spite of the buck Der-ry down down

down der-ry down

Come, all Yankee soldiers, give ear to my song,
It is a short ditty, 'twill not keep you long;
It's of no use to fret on account of our luck,
We can laugh, drink, and sing yet in spite of the buck.
Derry down, down, down, derry down.

"Sergeant, buck him and gag him," our officers cry,
For each trifling offense which they happen to spy,
Till with bucking and gagging of Dick, Pat, and Bill,
Faith, the Mexican's ranks they have helped to fill.
Derry down, down, down, derry down.

The treatment they give us, as all of us know,
Is bucking and gagging for whipping the foe;
They buck us and gag us for malice or spite,
But they are glad to release us when going to fight.
Derry down, down, down, derry down.

A poor soldier's tied up in the hot sun or rain,
With a gag in his mouth till he's tortured with pain,
Why, I'm blessed if the eagle we wear on our flag,
In its claws shouldn't carry a buck and a gag.
Derry down, down down, derry down.

busco would have fallen much sooner if it had not been for the artillery company of deserters. Knowing the ultimate punishment they faced for joining the Mexican side, the deserters put up the most desperate resistance rather than surrender.

How had American soldiers come to this terrible moment?

The story begins early in the war, in April 1846, when General Zachary Taylor arrived on the bank of the Rio Grande. The Mexicans tried propaganda on the American troops before they turned to guns. They knew many of Taylor's men were foreign-born and Catholic. A tide of Irish immigration had begun in the 1820s, prodded by crop failures and the heavy boot of Britain's colonial rule. The desperately poor immigrants, with their strange brogues and their Catholicism, became the victims of prejudice and contempt at the hands of native-born Americans. Despairing of winning acceptance and decent jobs, some Irish migrated to the Far West while others sought refuge in the regular army.

Intensified hostility early in the 1840s made the Irish targets of a powerful Native American or "Know Nothing" movement that opposed voting and officeholding rights for Catholics and the foreign-born. In May 1844 and again in July of that year, the agitation climaxed in bloody riots at Philadelphia. Armed mobs had sacked and burned Roman Catholic churches and schools.

The Mexicans tried to take advantage of these divisions among their enemy. Mexican generals peppered Taylor's troops with proclamations in English charging the Americans were carrying out a Masonic plot against the Catholic church and urging all good Catholics to desert. Anyone who deserted was promised 320 acres of land and Mexican citizenship.

Taylor was astonished at how many of his men responded to the Mexican appeals, even before the shooting began. A Sergeant John Riley—once a drillmaster at West Point—was the first to desert. The Mexicans welcomed him with a commission as lieutenant. Enough American soldiers followed him to make up a San Patricio Battalion. It fought in the defense of Monterrey. Upon the appeal of Mexican priests, some fifty more soldiers in Taylor's occupation force deserted. All were regular army men; not a single volunteer went over to the Mexicans, even though almost over a third of the volunteers were Catholics. One reason for the volunteers' resistance to Mexican propaganda may have been the assassination by Mexicans of Father Rey, a popular Jesuit priest attached to the volunteer units.

The San Patricio Battalion fought again at Buena Vista, functioning as artillerymen. When Santa Anna retreated, they marched to Mexico City where their strength was increased by other foreigners living in the capital.

While Scott's army prepared at Puebla for the advance on Mexico City, the enemy elaborated another plan to induce mass desertion of the 3,000 Catholics in the American ranks. The basic offer was a bonus of $10 and 200 acres of land to all deserters. The cash prize rose if a soldier came in with his weapons or a friend. Deserters were promised they could form companies of their own. The proclamation addressed them as "Sons of Ireland, a noble race," and asked:

Can you fight by the side of those who put fire to your temples in Boston and Philadelphia? Come over to us! May Mexicans and Irishmen, united by the sacred ties of religion and benevolence, form only one people.

This appeal failed to bring the wholesale desertion the Mexicans hoped for, but about two hundred men did go over to the Mexican side. All were added to the San Patricio Battalion.

General Scott retaliated by recruiting the prisoners in Puebla's town jail. He offered freedom to all who would join in a special company of mounted Mexican scouts. The twenty-two convicted men who chose to fight against their own people rather than remain in jail were put under the command of Dominguez, a condemned murderer. Called Dominguez's Scouts, the men proved useful to Scott because of their familiarity with the terrain.

It was the San Patricios at Churubusco who gave the Americans the most stubborn resistance they would meet in the entire war. Their defense of a bridge near the convent of San Pueblo cost Scott's troops heavy losses. Finally it took hand-to-hand fighting to subdue the 260 Patricios. Riley and scores of others were taken prisoner; the rest were either killed or escaped.

A court-martial a few days later tried twenty-nine prisoners. They were convicted and sentenced to be hanged. But upon review of each man's case, General Scott commuted the sentences of seven men. Instead of death, said his General Order No. 340, they were

to forfeit all pay and allowances, to receive fifty lashes each on the bare back, well laid on, to have the letter

General Wool informs mutineers of their fate.

D indelibly branded on the cheek with a red-hot iron, to be confined at hard labor, wearing about the neck an iron collar having three prongs each six inches long, the whole weighing eight pounds, for six months, and at the expiration of that time to have the head shaved and be drummed out of the service.

In addition, Scott pardoned two men because he was satisfied they had been captured and forced into the battalion, and had refused to fight.

News of the sentences imposed on the deserters upset the Mexicans. To Ramírez, for instance, they were not traitors but "the generous foreign soldiers," and other Mexicans called them "the Irish Martyrs." The archbishop of Mexico and many prominent Mexicans begged Scott for clemency while the ladies of the capital sent him petitions for mercy.

Scott would let nothing change his decision. On September 10, he had the sentences carried out at San Angel. Colonel George Davis told how it was done:

Those that were to be whipped and branded were tied up to trees in front of the Catholic church on the plaza, their backs naked . . . and an experienced Mexican muleteer inflicted the fifty lashes with all the severity he could upon each culprit. Why those thus punished did not die under such punishment was a marvel to me. Their backs had the appearance of a pounded piece of raw beef, the blood oozing from every stripe as given. Each in his turn was then branded and forced to dig the graves of those subsequently hung.

Sixteen of the San Patricios, wearing the Mexican uniforms they had been captured in, and with white hoods placed over their heads, were taken to the gallows. Eight carts drawn by pairs of mules were lined up evenly, and on the rear end of each, two condemned men were stood, nooses around their necks. A drum tapped an even beat, the carts moved forward, and sixteen bodies swung in the air, all life gone.

The four remaining of this group were hanged from a tree the next day at the village of Mixcoac.

Another court-martial tried the remaining deserters, thirty-six men. All were convicted and sentenced to death by hanging. After review, General Scott remitted the sentence of two men and commuted that of four others to lashing and branding. The other thirty he ordered to be hanged at Mixcoac on the day his army would storm Chapultepec Castle.

The deserters spared execution worked out their sentences at hard labor during the American occupation of Mexico City. The last we hear of them is a newspaper report in May 1848 which said the men were to be shipped to New Orleans where they would be dishonorably discharged.

15

THE HALLS OF MONTEZUMA

"Everything, everything has been lost, except our honor. That was lost a long time ago," wrote José Fernando Ramírez the day after the disasters of Contreras and Churubusco. In Mexico City, he said:

No one can talk of anything but the horrible misfortune and that, to cap the climax, everybody, including the troops themselves, believes that Santa Anna betrayed us. I cannot bring myself to think this, because it is my firm conviction that the whole affair can be explained clearly as being the result of the incompetence and cowardice of our generals and our leaders who, with the exception of Valencia and some of those with him, have given proof of what they have been, are, and will continue to be: cowards, ignoramuses, and men wholly devoid of even one spark of personal honor.

With dispirited troops and a demoralized citizenry, Santa Anna badly needed time. Scott, too, felt that his tired army needed rest. The Americans knew the Mexican capital was in confusion and that many were ready to give up peacefully. But if Scott entered the city now, it would wound Mexican pride and drive the government out, perhaps delaying any chance for peace. He sent word asking for a surrender; Santa Anna countered with a request for a brief armistice during which generals and diplomats could negotiate a peace. Terms for an armistice were therefore established on August 24, 1847. Neither side was to strengthen its position while peace negotiations took place.

Many American troops thought Scott was mistaken in agreeing to an armistice. After the successes of Contreras and Churubusco, they believed they could easily take Mexico City. As it turned out, Scott weakened his position relatively by giving the enemy a breather. Santa Anna reorganized his army, put thousands of troops to digging ditches and throwing up earth fortifications day and night. When, contrary to the terms of the armistice, he let a crowd attack an American wagon train entering the city to buy forage and provisions, Scott was furious. Meanwhile, negotiations for a peace were producing no results. On September 6 Scott notified Santa Anna that he was ending the armistice.

The situation inside Mexico City, at this moment, is pictured by Ramírez:

The city presents an imposing aspect that becomes terrible at times. The church bells, which have been silent for many days, ring only to spread the alarm; and this sound of church bells, which produces feverish excitement in the streets and public squares, is followed by the silence of desolation, because half the inhabitants crowd the rooftops to see what their fate may be, while the other half lock themselves indoors or rush to arms to prepare to defend themselves to the last.

The next day Scott moved his troops up to Tacubaya, on the approach to the city's southwestern defenses. Two strong points lay ahead. One was the castle of Chapultepec, now used as a military college. It was a strong stone building on top of a rocky hill, wooded from the base about halfway up. Because it commanded the entrance to the city on that side, it was essential to take it. Half a mile west of the castle was a cluster of stone buildings known as Molino del Rey, or King's Mill, which housed the country's biggest iron foundry. Cannon and gunpowder were said to be turned out daily there. Scott decided it was important to seize the Molino first in order to destroy the military stores.

Shortly before sunrise on September 8 Scott began the attack on Molino. The troops moved in on the southernmost buildings first, but were forced back by destructive fire which left the field covered with American dead and wounded. "The Mexican lancers," said a bitter Private Ballentine, "exhibited most characteristically both their cowardice and cruelty of disposition on this occasion, by riding out and killing the wounded who were lying on the field, while they never attempted to follow up the broken line of infantry who had been compelled to retire."

Then Scott tried the enemy's center, a stone building called Casa Mata. Again he suffered heavy losses and had to move back and leave it to the artillery to reduce the strong position. On the far right there was a duel of cavalry forces which ended when an American charge broke through the Mexican line.

By seven in the morning the fighting was over. In a letter to his father, Captain John Sedgwick told what had happened to himself and his friends during the assault on the Molino:

The loss on our side was irreparable; many of our most gallant officers and soldiers fell. I had a very narrow escape: a ball struck me on the shoulder and knocked me down, but did not disable me for a minute. An officer of my regiment, and a classmate, was blown up in the magazine after the fight was over. He had charge of renewing the ammunition, and after taking most of it out he asked permission to blow up the rest, which was granted. He laid the train, but, it not going off as soon as he expected, he returned to see the cause, and was blown up with it.

American losses were heavy: 117 killed, 658 wounded, and 18 missing out of some 3,500 men. And the result? Inside the mill Scott found nothing—no cannon, no military stores. Everything had already been removed to the city. "A sad mistake," wrote Colonel Hitchcock in his diary. A few more such victories and Scott's small army would be wiped out. Still, he took comfort from the fact that Santa Anna had suffered another defeat. All that day, said Ramírez, inside the capital "there was constant excitement, with a ringing of bells that became unbearable. . . . This ringing . . . filled the entire city with terror, causing some people to go about shouting that the enemy was already in the city."

Holding council with his staff, Scott asked them which route they should take into the capital. He looked first to Captain Robert E. Lee of the engineers. Lee's advice, to make an approach from the south, was favored by several other officers. But Pierre Beauregard, another young engineer, spoke for a group that wanted to take the western route through the fortress of Chapultepec. After the possibilities were debated, Scott said, "Gentlemen, we will attack by the western gates." He sent Pillow and Quitman to create a diversion at the eastern side, with orders to abandon the position on the night of September 12.

Chapultepec had been readied for an assault all through the summer and now was under the command of General Nicolas Bravo. But because Santa Anna was confident the Americans would make their heaviest attack at the eastern gate, he left Bravo with too few troops.

On the morning of September 12 the artillery began a bombardment of the castle that lasted all day and through the night. Under cover of darkness Scott moved his troops into position. The relentless pounding wore down Bravo's men. He asked for reinforcements. Santa Anna promised him fresh troops, but not until the decisive moment.

At daylight on September 13 cannonading began again as three divisions prepared to attack from different points—Quitman's from the south, Pillow's from the southwest, and Worth's from the extreme west. At eight o'clock the army attacked in force. The fighting was intense, the American troops hampered by the failure to have scaling ladders in the right place when needed. Santa Anna never got the replacements to Bravo, and much of Chapultepec's defense was fought by the cadets of the military college.

The assignment of Private Ballentine's battery was to get to the bottom of the hill of Chapultepec and

Storming the castle at Chapultepec.

throw shells and round shot into the wood and up the face of the hill to prepare the way for Scott's assault troops. This is how the private saw the storming of the castle:

Shortly after sunrise we received orders to commence firing. An ill-directed fire of musketry from the enemy's outlying piquets stationed in the woods, reached us as we commenced firing, slightly wounding several of our men. But a few shells thrown in the right direction soon removed that source of annoyance, and where we were the guns of the castle could not be depressed sufficiently to bear on us. We continued to fire until we had thrown over a hundred shots into the grounds, when we were told to cease firing and allow the infantry to advance. To get into the grounds they had to scale a wall about six or seven feet high, and with the aid of the ladders they were soon all over. . . .

While the infantry advanced on the castle we hitched the horses into the battery and stood waiting to pursue the enemy, who we were confident would not make a long resistance, as the bombardment of the previous day had done great execution on the building. The firing from the castle soon commenced on our assaulting party, who at first suffered severely, but after about two hours' hard fighting, they scaled the steep ascent and drove the enemy from the ramparts. General Bravo and several hundred of the Mexican soldiers were taken prisoner in the castle. [The cadets, only boys, had fought with great courage. Some of them chose now to jump from the cliffs to their death rather than surrender.] *The remainder of the garrison escaped by the opposite side of the*

castle from which our troops entered, and ran in con-
fusion along the highway to the city.

By 9:30 A.M. the Mexicans were forced to surrender. The Americans had taken the last major barrier to the capital, at a cost of about 500 casualties. The Mexican dead, wounded, and captured amounted to some 1,800 men.

This time Scott allowed no breathing space. He ordered the troops to move rapidly on the gates of the city, Quitman's division going along the causeway to the Belen Gate and Worth's by the San Cosmé Gate. All along the route the artillery did deadly work in eliminating pockets of resistance. The Mexican troops could not stand up against the onslaught and fled together with many of their generals. By early afternoon Quitman had planted an American flag on the city wall. Worth's men reached the San Cosmé Gate about four o'clock. Held up there by heavy fire, they burrowed under the adobe houses lining the road and reached the rear of the enemy. Then they lifted howitzers to a housetop overlooking the Mexican batteries and drove the astonished enemy off with their fire. By six o'clock in the evening, Worth had his gate.

The day's fighting had worn down the small American army and cost them 900 men. Supplies and ammunition were dangerously low as they contemplated the costly task of capturing the city block by block from a much larger army defending its own capital.

In the first hours of that night Santa Anna seemed to be rallying his forces for the defense. He had 5,000 infantry placed inside the fortified Citadel, and another

not help remembering then the description by Prescott of Cortez's flight from this city during the celebrated "Noche Triste" about 317 years before—by the very road I was then travelling upon. It seemed to me that every moment I would hear the demoniacal yell of his savage and infuriated foes, when they suddenly discovered his retreat and commenced their deadly attack upon him.

The next days in the capital were a hell for both sides. The heavy fighting had left the American troops in a savage state of mind. Looting and rape were common. Mexican snipers were everywhere. If an American walked in the streets alone, he was likely never to get back to his company. The undercover struggle that went on is conveyed by Ramírez in a letter he wrote two weeks after Mexico City was taken:

Our enemy is oppressing and humiliating us. How I would like to bring home this lesson to certain politicians who have talked incessantly about despotism! Here they would see and get a taste of what it means to live without guarantees! It is all so frightful. I must say that those who have conquered us, brutally savage as they are, have conducted themselves in a manner different from that of European armies belonging to nations that bear the standard of civilization. This does not mean that they do not commit countless excesses every day. But we have here a phenomenon consisting of mingled barbarism and restraint. This has been the situation for several days, and there is no way to account for it. . . .

The plague has begun to show its signs, and the monuments these filthy soldiers have scattered along the streets of their quarters unmistakably testify to the fact that dysentery is destroying them. I have never before seen such sodden drunkenness, nor any more scandalous or impudent than the drunkenness that holds these men in its grip. Nor have I ever seen more unrestrained appetites. Every hour of the day, except during the evenings, when they are all drunk, one can find them eating everything they see.

The Palace and almost all public buildings have been savagely ransacked and destroyed. I think it only right to say, however, that our disgraceful rabble were the ones who began it all. When the enemy's troops entered the Palace, the doors had already been broken down and the building had been plundered. Three days later the embroidered velvet canopy was sold for four pesos at the Palace entrance. The infamous and eternally accursed Santa Anna abandoned us all, both individuals and property, to the mercy of the enemy and did not leave even one sentinel to defend us.

At last the guerrilla fighting ceased, Scott recovered control of his men, and the Mexicans sank into sullen acceptance of the occupation. Scott put the city under martial law, guaranteeing the people their safety, property, and religion. The Mexican courts began to sit again, the shops opened up, newspapers started printing, and soon the American soldiers were relieving the boredom of occupation duty by their usual entertainments.

Crushed by his defeats, Santa Anna resigned the presidency. Toward the end of September he tried to recapture Puebla but was driven off easily. His command was taken away from him in October, and a court-mar-

U.S. troops in the grand plaza, Mexico City.

tial was launched to investigate his conduct of the war. In the end the government banished him, and he left for Jamaica.

Pedro María Anaya was elected interim president of Mexico. The new government wanted to make peace quickly, before the Americans could do even more damage to Mexico as a nation. It informed the Americans that commissioners stood ready to negotiate peace on the basis of the original terms. Mexico's moderates— able to foresee the outcome of the war—had been for peace from the beginning. As Justo Sierra put it, "Even before the annexation of Texas, peace was urgent; after that, imperative; after the war, our only salvation." As for the accusations of the political opposition that to make peace was to sell out the country and lose all honor, Sierra said:

The principle that a country must never cede territory is absurd, and no country, once invaded and conquered, has been able to sustain it. The true principle is quite different: a country in the grip of dire necessity can and should cede a part of its territory in order to conserve the rest.

16

ALL MEXICO!

Who would negotiate the peace? And what kind of peace would it be?

Back in April, as General Scott was beginning his advance inland from Vera Cruz, President Polk had found the man to make the peace. He was Nicholas P. Trist, chief clerk of the State Department, a Virginian and a staunch member of the Democratic party. Polk wanted Trist to accompany Scott's army so that he could seize any chance to open negotiations. Scott himself might have been given this task, for he had shown skill in diplomacy during his long career. But the general was a Whig and a presidential hopeful. The administration preferred to entrust the important task to a Democrat.

Scott had hoped to cap his military triumph by negotiating the peace himself. He resented Trist's arrival on the scene, the more so when he learned that Trist carried the draft of a proposed basic treaty which he was not to let Scott see. Trist had also been given authority to tell Scott when to suspend military action so that Trist could negotiate. Put in this position, Scott felt degraded and warned Trist to keep out of military affairs. He considered Trist a pompous, conceited clerk playing the role of spy for Polk. Trist in turn thought Scott "decidedly the greatest imbecile that I have ever had anything to do with." The two men quarreled so bitterly they stopped talking.

Taken sick for two months, Trist softened and let Scott read the official documents he had come with. Polk had instructed Trist to demand California and New Mexico, and to stipulate that the Rio Grande should be the border between Texas and Mexico and to offer no more than $30 million for that territory. A reconciliation took place between Trist and Scott and from then on the two men worked together. Perhaps the discovery of a mutual distaste for Polk helped cement their friendship.

Operating through the British legation, Trist began negotiations with the Mexican government in June, while Scott's army was at Puebla. The Mexicans turned down his proposals. But as they suffered one defeat after another, they became more amenable. Trist played a role in Scott's decision to offer Santa Anna the bribe he asked to end the war; and again in August, during the armistice negotiations that followed the battle of Churubusco, Trist was important. After that second failure, Trist and Scott agreed that a peace would come only after Mexico had been totally defeated.

When the Americans occupied Mexico City it appeared that the time had come. The enemy's capital, her chief port, New Mexico, Upper California—all were in American hands. Her armies were scattered, her treasury empty. Such a hopeless situation would warrant an unconditional surrender. But that did not happen, for several reasons. The Mexicans were a proud people

Nicholas Trist.

and refused to admit defeat. Scott's army of occupation was so small they hoped it would not be able to hold the capital for long. The liberals did not want the generals to make the peace because it would only extend their grip on the state. And finally, if negotiations could be stalled, antiwar forces inside the United States might be able to bring about a peace on terms more favorable to Mexico.

Mexico carried on negotiations, said Polk, as though her armies had won. She proposed terms he considered utterly impossible, including a flat refusal to cede New Mexico and California. Under steady fire from the Whig opposition, the President got tougher. By October, he determined to get even more out of Mexico and to give even less for it. He wanted the enemy to pay for prolonging the war. He instructed Trist to tell the Mexicans they must now come to Washington to negotiate. Trist was to break off any talks he might have begun with the Mexicans and come home at once.

In the six weeks it took for that message to reach Trist, Mexico City fell, Santa Anna was in disgrace, and a new government was showing a warmer interest in coming to terms. Trist was ready to take advantage of this change when Polk's instructions arrived. What should he do? Go home as ordered, or stay and work out a treaty?

With Scott's encouragement and the approval of the British chargé, Edward Thornton, Trist took the risk of disobeying his orders. He believed if he were to leave now, the peace party in Mexico might lose control to the belligerents. He concluded the Polk administration was too remote to appreciate the situation at this critical moment. It was therefore his duty not to lose this chance, but to try to make a treaty on his own.

Trist calculated that Polk would be forced to accept a treaty because the country had grown so sick of the war. He sent the President a sixty-page letter justifying his actions. When the angry Polk had waded through the ocean of words he emerged on the far shore denouncing Trist as an "impudent and unqualified scoundrel" and ordered him again to return home.

On December 28, 1847, the Mexican commissioners met with Trist at the town of Guadalupe Hidalgo, a few miles north of the capital. It was fortunate that Trist acted as he had, and that the Mexicans were now ready to negotiate. For in the United States, a movement to demand *all* Mexico had built to threatening size.

The victories of both Taylor's and Scott's armies had given renewed enthusiasm to the followers of Manifest Destiny. Now they were raising the cry of "All Mexico!" Each military success whetted their appetite for more territory. It took on the fervor of a religious revival. A new strain was the notion that America had a sacred duty to regenerate the unfortunate Mexicans by absorbing them into our great democracy. Providence, said Moses Y. Beach, editor of the *New York Sun*, had "willed the Mexican War to unite and exalt both nations." On October 22, soon after Mexico City was taken, he wrote of the Mexicans:

The race is perfectly accustomed to being conquered, and the only new lesson we shall teach is that our victories will give liberty, safety and prosperity to the van-

quished, if they know enough to profit by the appearance of our stars. To liberate and ennoble—not to enslave and debase—is our mission. Well may the Mexican nation, whose great masses have never yet tasted liberty, prattle over their lost phantom of nationality. . . . If they have not—in the profound darkness of their vassal existence—the intelligence and manhood to accept the ranks and rights of freemen at our hands, we must bear with their ignorance.

That same day the *Times*, Boston's most widely read paper, assured Mexico it was a blessing for her to be conquered by the Americans:

The "conquest" which carries peace into a land where the sword has always been the sole arbiter between factions equally base, which institutes the reign of law where license has existed for a generation; which provides for the education and elevation of the great mass of the people, who have, for a period of 300 years, been the helots of an overbearing foreign race, and which causes religious liberty, and full freedom of mind to prevail where a priesthood has long been enabled to prevent all religion save that of its worship—such a "conquest," stigmatize it as you please, must necessarily be a great blessing to the conquered.

No longer were the expansionists concerned only with self-aggrandizement. The conquest of land was to be morally redeemed by the regeneration of its inhabitants. As Walt Whitman had said when he advocated that America take California, it would cause an "increase of human happiness and liberty." Even the anti-

Commemorative medal voted to Scott by Congress.

war magazine *New Englander* began to think "this war may result in great good to the world—to this country —to Mexico herself—to the cause of learning, good government, and religion."

To any argument based on the "superiority of race," Albert Gallatin had a sharp reply. Swiss by birth and American by choice, Gallatin had served his adopted country as a statesman and diplomat. When the Mexican War broke out he was eighty-five, but his age did not weaken his outspoken opposition. As a pioneer ethnologist, he had no patience with racist excuses for the war. In his 1847 book, *Peace With Mexico*, he said:

The allegation that the subjugation of Mexico would be the means of enlightening the Mexicans, of improving their social state, and of increasing their happiness, is but the shallow attempt to disguise unbounded cupidity and ambition.

But more effective than the learned Gallatin was that tongue-in-cheek oracle, "Major Jack Downing." The immensely popular character of Downing, who posed as the Yankee friend of Presidents, was created by Seba Smith, a newspaperman from Maine. Letters signed by Jack Downing were reprinted all over the country. Now, reflecting on the way the war with Mexico was going, the major said:

The long and short of it is, we fit our way into the City of Mexico and annexed it. Santa Anna cleared out the night afore with what troops he had left, and is scouring about the country to get some more places ready for us to annex. When he gets another place all ready for the ceremony, and gets it well fortified, and has an army of twenty or thirty thousand men in the forts and behind the breastworks, we shall march down upon 'em with five or six thousand men, and go through the flurry. After they have shot down about half of us, the rest of us will climb in, over the mouths of their cannons, and annex that place; and so on, one after another. It's pretty hard work annexin' in this way but it's the only way it can be done. It will be necessary for the President to keep hurryin' on his men to keep our ranks full, for we've got a great deal of ground to go over yet. What we've annexed in Mexico so far, isn't a circumstance to what we've got to do. . . . It's dangerous standin' still in this annexin' business. It's like the old woman's soap—if it don't go ahead it goes back.

By December, as Trist's negotiations dragged on, almost every editor was asking, "What shall we do with Mexico?" The *Philadelphia Public Ledger*'s reply was typical of many:

We cannot let go without disgrace. Her fools can resist us no longer, and her wise are imploring our protection against the fools. We cannot back out entirely; we cannot take part and leave the rest. We have got the whole and must do something with it.

The principle of indemnity colored the argument. The longer the state of war lasted, the more the defeated power should be made to pay in territory. In January 1848 the New York State Democratic Convention resolved:

That the title of the Mexican government is a title

by conquest from those who held it by conquest. If we took it and held it by the same title, they could not complain. Their title is legal; and our title would also be legal.

Three prominent members of Polk's administration —Secretary of State Buchanan, Secretary of the Treasury Walker, and Vice President Dallas—echoed this demand for annexing all Mexico. Polk himself in his annual message of December 7, 1847, said that the provinces of California and New Mexico now occupied by American troops should be taken over as partial indemnity at once. No treaty was needed for that. And all the other parts of Mexico in the Army's hands should remain under military control until peace is made. The peace, he said, must include "indemnity for the past and security for the future."

What the President meant by that last balanced phrase was plain to some people. As one wit told the Senate, "Indemnity for the past means half of Mexico, and security for the future, the other half."

Those who hungered for all Mexico had more than moral considerations in mind. Cortez himself, three hundred years earlier, had first suggested the potential of a man-made passage across the Isthmus of Tehuantepec. During the Mexican War that was the favorite among several routes proposed by advocates of an interoceanic canal. Now that the United States had pocketed Oregon and California, great commercial benefits could be gained from such a link with the Far West. Promoters of trade were equally concerned with building a rail connection between East and West. One of the routes proposed for a transcontinental railroad would head south and pass through lands now Mexican. The expansionists saw the chance for realizing both dreams through a settlement with Mexico at the peace table.

In the 30th Congress which assembled in December 1847, the issue of All Mexico was debated openly for the first time. To the amazement of many, Senator John C. Calhoun of South Carolina at once took the lead in opposing imperialist expansion. His speeches against the acquisition of all Mexico produced "a bombshell in every quarter," reported the *New York Herald*. The voice of the proslavery Democrats was now on the same side as that of the Whigs who had raised the original clamor against Democratic imperialism. But some of those same antislavery Whigs, as we have seen, were now eager to secure all the territory in the Southwest that was possible.

What had brought about such switches?

To both Calhoun and the editors of the abolitionist *National Era* the issue of slavery was all-important. Each now understood that Mexico was economically unsuited to slavery and that its people and its states were unalterably opposed to the institution. American absorption of Mexico would therefore harm the slavery interest. Plainly, then, Calhoun had to oppose the expansionist movement. Annexation of Mexico would add free states to the Union and tip the balance of power against the slave states.

Besides, extending citizenship to the colored people of Mexico was abhorrent to Calhoun, a vigorous racist. In January 1848 he said in the Senate:

John C. Calhoun.

I know further, sir, that we have never dreamt of incorporating into our Union any but the Caucasian race —the free white race. To incorporate Mexico, would be the very first instance of the kind, of incorporating an Indian race; for more than half the Mexicans are Indians, and the other is composed chiefly of mixed tribes. I protest against such a union as that! Ours, sir, is the Government of a white race. The greatest misfortunes of Spanish America are to be traced to the fatal error of placing these colored races in an equality with the white race. . . .

Precisely because Calhoun and the proslavery Democrats held such views, wrote the *National Era* of February 3, "we must be pardoned for dwelling with pleasure upon the extension of our territory and the expansion of our population." Even if all Mexico were annexed, the editorial said, the antislavery interests had nothing to fear. Calhoun's opposition was proof of that.

But by the time the *National Era* took up the cry for All Mexico, the issue had been settled. The negotiations for peace had been going on for two months. The Mexican side labored under great difficulties—military, political, and personal rivalries complicated making any decision. And above all, a treaty to the liking of Americans would be hateful and humiliating to Mexicans. Still, there was the implicit threat that if the American demands were impossibly harsh, Mexico would sink into anarchy and a guerrilla war would make occupation hell for the Americans indefinitely.

Trist, too, was burdened by heavy anxiety. He was negotiating illegally and at any moment might find himself arrested on Polk's orders. His bargaining position, of course, was powerful. He represented the conqueror, whose army stood poised to move again should the negotiations fail.

On February 2, 1848 peace terms were signed by both sides at Guadalupe Hidalgo. By their provisions New Mexico and Upper California were ceded to the United States, and all claims to Texas were relinquished by the Mexicans. The U.S.–Mexican boundary was fixed along the lower Rio Grande, from its mouth to El Paso, thence westward along New Mexico's southern border to its western end, then north to the Gila River, along that river to where it met the Colorado, and finally along the line between Upper and Lower California to the Pacific Ocean.

The Mexicans had begged for an article in the treaty banning slavery in the ceded territories. No, said Trist; even to mention that subject was out of the question. Multiply the territory ten times in value, he said, overlay it a foot thick with gold, on the single condition that slavery should not be permitted in it, and it would still be impossible for him to communicate such a proposition to the President.

By the agreement the United States acquired 850,000 square miles—about one-third of Mexico's land. It was more than the combined area of France, Spain, and Italy. It was the minimum Trist had been instructed in April to accept. Mexicans who lived in the ceded areas were eligible for American citizenship. The United States paid $15 million for the cession and assumed claims of its citizens against Mexico for $3.25 million more.

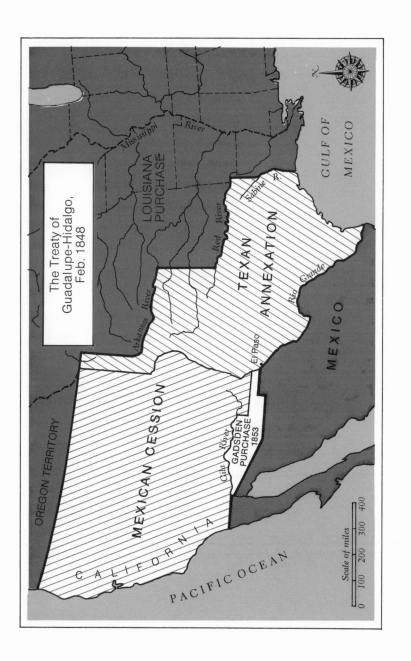

The Treaty of
Guadalupe-Hidalgo,
Feb. 1848

OREGON TERRITORY

LOUISIANA
PURCHASE

Mississippi   River

Red   River

Arkansas   River

TEXAN

ANNEXATION

Sabine R.

Rio Grande

El Paso

MEXICAN CESSION

Gila   River

GADSDEN
PURCHASE
1853

CALIFORNIA

MEXICO

GULF OF
MEXICO

PACIFIC OCEAN

Scale of miles
0   100   200   300   400

The treaty reached Washington on February 19. Polk and his cabinet were still angered by Trist's extraordinary behavior, but the country was in no mood to see the treaty thrown out. The House had just passed by a vote of 85 to 81 a resolution branding the war as "unnecessary and unconstitutional."

Even before the text of the treaty had reached Washington, when its terms were only rumor, Horace Greeley had written in his *New York Tribune*:

> As to the presumed Treaty, we hope the Senate will ratify anything Mr. Polk may send them, even in the sneaking underhand fashion of his Oregon Treaty. Peace! Peace! even though we pay Fifteen Millions of Dollars for it and take a thousand miles of inhospitable deserts haunted by implacably hostile savages as a consideration, in order that Polk & Co. may boast of their conquests and annexations. Sign anything, ratify anything, pay anything, to end the guilt, the bloodshed, the shame, the enormous waste of this horrible contest.

Polk decided to submit this treaty to the Senate. It was pretty much what he had told Trist to get last April. To demand more would mean resuming the fighting which would only intensify the criticism of his administration. Even in his own party, men like Calhoun were leading a revolt against taking more of Mexico. If he rejected a treaty whose terms he had once approved, the Whigs, who now held the purse strings in Congress, might deny him the funds needed to extend the war, and charge him with wanting all along to grab all Mexico. Polk knew, too, that people were tired of taxes to meet the heavy financial burden of the war. "The luxury of conquest," complained Edward Everett, was costing the country a total of about $100 million. And uppermost in Polk's mind was the political calendar: the next presidential campaign was almost at hand. Better settle the peace now than risk losing the election of 1848.

After a debate which showed a desire to make only a few minor changes, the Senate voted on ratification of the treaty. It was approved, 38 to 14. In favor were 26 Democrats and 12 Whigs; against were 7 Democrats and 7 Whigs. (A motion to add the Wilmot Proviso to the treaty was beaten, 38 to 15.) Most of the opposition came from those who wanted to annex all Mexico. A final territorial adjustment under the treaty came in 1853 when James Gadsden negotiated with Mexico for cession of a rectangular strip of land in the Mesilla Valley, south of the Gila River, desired by the United States as a southern railroad route to the Pacific. The Gadsden Purchase price was $10 million.

The Mexican Congress ratified the treaty in May, and Polk proclaimed it in effect in July. The public and both political parties expressed their satisfaction. The All Mexico movement collapsed.

17

FROM COMPROMISE
TO CIVIL WAR

It was midsummer 1848—ten months after the fighting
ended—before Jacob Oswandel, now promoted to cor-
poral, saw his home again. On Monday, July 24, the
train bearing his First Regiment, Pennsylvania Volunteers, was chugging through the countryside on its way
into Philadelphia. At every station along the road the
people gathered to welcome the soldiers home, he said:

*Salutes were fired and cheering all along the road,
and when we arrived in sight of Philadelphia, we could
see the thousands of people and hear the roaring of artillery. At the foot of the inclined plane we were met
by one mass of people, cheering, and all seemed full of
enthusiasm. The tops of the cars, and platforms and all
along the railroad was crowded with people.*

*About 10 o'clock, A.M., we formed into line and
marched through the whole volunteer division. The
streets and sidewalks were so densely crowded that it
was almost impossible to get along.*

In fact, guards were stationed on our route of march-

ing to keep the people from crowding in on us, so anxious were they to see the soldiers of the Mexican war.

The business was generally suspended, and all the houses along the route were crowded with spectators, and beautifully decorated with flowers and flags. After marching through several of the principal streets, we marched into the Chinese Museum and sat down to one of the grandest dinners that ever was provided for distinguished guests. The best of edibles and the choicest of all the best wines. Speeches were made and songs sung by the citizens. . . .

In the evening the veterans were treated to a huge fireworks display in the center of the city, "really magnificent and indescribable." Worn out by the day's celebration, the soldiers were at last allowed to go to bed. Oswandel's mind turned to the fate of the men he had joined up with back in January 1847. His Company C had spent about nine months in action and another nine months on occupation duty. When their service began, the company had been made up of 12 commissioned and noncommissioned officers and 81 privates. "C" had come home with 10 officers and 35 privates. Of the remainder, 2 men had been transferred out, 7 had deserted, 15 had died, 22 had been discharged during the war, and 2 he could not account for.

The United States had grown enormously through this war. Now attention turned to how the new territories should be organized. Would they be open to free labor alone? Or would the southerners have an equal chance to bring in their slaves, against whom free labor could not compete? It was a fundamental issue that faced both parties as they prepared for their national conventions in the summer of 1848.

The dissent expressed during the war revealed the sectional conflicts that had begun to strain the bonds of union and to break apart both major parties. Only three months after the war had begun, antislavery men had introduced the Wilmot Proviso in a campaign to keep new territories free. The proviso was still before the country. Southerners knew that if Congress ever adopted it, the spread of slavery would be checked and the political power of the slave states doomed. They denied Congress's right to interfere with slavery in the territories. They argued that the territories were the common possession of all Americans. The constitutional duty of Congress was to protect slave property in the territories. Only a territory itself, when it achieved statehood, could forbid slavery, the southerners insisted.

These were basic questions, questions not settled by the war but opened up by it. They became the issues of the 1848 election that immediately followed the signing of the peace.

The Democrats wrote a platform that defended the war as "just and necessary." It took the position that Congress could not interfere with slavery in the states. Efforts by antislavery men in the party to introduce the Wilmot Proviso at the Democratic convention were cut off. Polk, who had pledged himself to a single term in the 1844 campaign, refused to run. The Democrats chose General Lewis Cass of Michigan, with General William O. Butler of Kentucky as his running mate. Cass was a militant expansionist whose position on

*Democratic cartoon attacking Taylor
in the election campaign of 1848.*

slavery was that the decision whether or not to introduce it should be left to the settlers themselves. This principle, of which Cass was the first advocate, became known as "popular sovereignty." It meant that the Democratic party was able to avoid taking a position on slavery's extension.

The Whig convention equivocated in the same way. It voted down a resolution to affirm the power of Congress to control slavery in the territories. The antislavery forces that backed it—the Northwest and the New Englanders—opposed the move to nominate General Zachary Taylor, owner of three hundred slaves. "Old Rough and Ready" had shown no interest in politics, never even bothering to vote. That lack of political principles coupled with his great popularity as the hero of the Mexican War endeared him to the President-makers. Tom Corwin, who dreamed of the Presidency himself, said Taylor's qualifications consisted of "sleeping forty years in the woods and cultivating moss on the calves of his legs." But the Whig convention wanted a winner, and General Taylor, silent on principles, was their man. They chose Millard Fillmore, a Buffalo politician, as his running mate, and presented the public, not with a platform, but with a song, "Rough and Ready."

Both political parties straddled the slavery issue in the Mexican territories. This gave the country a choice of Tweedledum or Tweedledee. The result was the emergence of a new party which had been taking form for some time. It was made up largely of antislavery Democrats and Conscience Whigs, plus the supporters of the older Liberty party. The Free Soil party offered a platform with something for everyone. It pleased the Liberty men by

Rough and Ready

Oh! There's not a can - vass go - ing worth show- ing or
know - ing like that from glo - ry grow - ing for our
"bold so - ger boy." A-way "Rough and read - y'll"
go soon you'll know friend or foe, the polls will quick- ly
show __ He's the "bold so - ger boy." There's
not a town he'll march thru but vo - ters look - ing
arch thru The ca - val - cade will sarch thru to
find the Na - tion's joy While in the street each

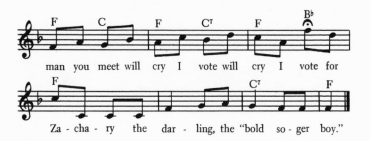

man you meet will cry I vote will cry I vote for Za - cha - ry the dar - ling, the "bold so - ger boy."

Oh, there's not a canvass going
Worth showing or knowing
Like that from glory growing
For our "bold soger boy."
Away Rough and Ready'll go
Soon you'll know friend or foe,
The polls will quickly show
He's our "bold soger boy."

There's not a town he'll march through,
But voters looking arch through,
The cavalcade will sarch through
To find the nation's joy.

While in the street,
Each man you meet
Will cry, "I vote,"
Will cry, "I vote
For Zachary, the darling,
The bold soger boy."

When the rest have got the rout
Oh! They'll pout and they'll shout
Then go right about
For the "bold soger boy."
When in the White House chair,
Won't that pair tear their hair
But he'll get there soft and fair,
Will our "bold soger boy."

Sure we see the game before us,
Though with "pledges" they may bore us,
All the people will encore us
And sing our songs with joy.
What's that we hear?
Repeat the cheer:
It's loud and clear
Hurrah! We shout
For Zachary, the darling,
The "bold soger boy."

endorsing the Wilmot Proviso; Westerners by demanding free homesteads for settlers; Whigs by supporting internal improvements; and Democrats by endorsing a tariff for revenue only, payment of the public debt, and cheap postage. On its banner it blazoned the slogan of "Free Soil, Free Speech, Free Labor, and Free Men." The Free Soilers nominated former President Martin Van Buren, a redeemed Democrat, with Charles Francis Adams, a converted Whig, for vice-president.

For the first time in a national election the whole country voted on the same day, November 7. Barely one-tenth of the population, now nearly 23 million, cast ballots. The result was close. Taylor drew 1,360,101 votes; Cass, 1,220,544. The electoral vote was 163 to 127.

Van Buren, with almost 300,000 votes, failed to win any state. But the Free Soilers helped elect Taylor by depriving Cass of New York's thirty-six electoral votes, exactly enough to have reversed the results had those votes gone to the Democrats. The Free Soilers elected thirteen candidates to the House of Representatives, giving them the balance of power between Whigs and Democrats. With a vote five times that cast for the Liberty party in 1844, the antislavery movement proved it had gained much ground in the last four years.

In March 1849 Polk rode to the inauguration in an open carriage with Taylor, and listened to the new President read his address. He shook Taylor's hand at the end of the ceremony and said, "I hope, Sir, the country may be prosperous under your administration." But Polk confided to his diary that the old soldier seemed to him to be of "very ordinary capacity" and

have resolved that the evil shall extend no farther. I say to the South in all frankness, you will find Northern sentiment immovable on the subject, "as firm as nature, and as fixed as fate."

Just as "immovable" had the southerners become. Robert Toombs of Georgia rose in the Congress in December 1849 to say:

I do not, then, hesitate to avow before this House and the country, and in the presence of the living God, that if by your legislation you seek to drive us from the territories of California and New Mexico, purchased by the common blood and treasure of the whole people, and to abolish slavery in this District, thereby attempting to fix a national degradation upon half the States of this Confederacy, I am for disunion; and if my physical courage be equal to the maintenance of my conviction of right and duty, I will devote all I am and all I have on earth to its consummation.

The threat of disunion, voiced often in the fevered debate, alarmed the great body of citizens. Could not some kind of give-and-take settle the issue and damp down the mounting sectional antagonism? It was Henry Clay, the Great Compromiser, who answered the appeal. Now seventy-three years old, the Kentuckian had returned to the Senate after an absence of seven years. He was committed to the preservation of the Union, and ready to conciliate the South to avoid a sectional clash. On January 29, 1850, he rose to offer the compromise he had devised.

First, Congress would admit California as a free state

Henry Clay.

while organizing Utah and New Mexico as territories without any restraint on slavery. Congress should induce Texas to surrender its extreme western boundary claims by offering to assume the Texas debt contracted before annexation. And finally, slave trading in the District of Columbia would be suppressed, but in return the South would be assured that there would be no interference with slavery itself in the District, or with the interstate slave trade, and that stronger measures for the return of fugitive slaves would be adopted.

Troubled though he was by a racking cough that had seized him in his advanced stage of tuberculosis, Clay took the Senate floor again a week later to support his compromise proposal. Washingtonians packed the gallery. He prayed the North to show forbearance and the South to have faith in the Union. Then he spoke on the threat of secession:

In my opinion there is no right on the part of any one or more of the States to secede from the Union. War and dissolution of the Union are identical and inevitable, in my opinion. There can be a dissolution of the Union only by consent or by war. Consent no one can anticipate, from any existing state of things, is likely to be given; and war is the only alternative by which a dissolution could be accomplished. . . . And such a war as it would be, following a dissolution of the Union! Sir, we may search the pages of history, and none so ferocious, so bloody, so implacable, so exterminating . . . I implore gentlemen, I adjure them, whether from the South or the North, to pause at the edge of the precipice, before the fearful and dangerous leap be taken

*into the yawning abyss below, from which none who
ever take it shall return in safety. . . .*

Like Clay, John C. Calhoun was nearing the end of
his career. He was so weak from a fatal illness he could
barely totter to his seat in the Senate on March 4, 1850,
the day he made his last defense of the rights of slaveholders. The public, sensing there would never be another appearance, crowded the Senate chamber. He
begged permission of the Chair, to have Senator James
M. Mason of Virginia read his speech because he had
not the strength to do it himself.

Sitting motionless as the speech was read, Calhoun
already seemed to be a voice from the grave. He would
have none of Clay's compromise. Rather disunion than
that. He knew the bonds of union, spiritual and political, were tearing apart. The abolitionist agitators were
solely to blame. He had little hope that dissolution
could be halted. The slave South, he reminded the Senate, was now being outnumbered in population and
political representation by the free North. To save the
Union, the North had to make concessions; the South
had none to make. California is the test case, he said.
If she is admitted as a free state, the North will show
it has the "intention of destroying, irretrievably, the
equilibrium between the two sections. We should be
blind not to perceive, in that case, that your actual,
your real objectives are power and aggrandizement, and
infatuated not to act accordingly." The only thing that
can preserve the South's rights, Calhoun said, is to
amend the Constitution so as to convert the govern-

ment into a federal alliance, in which the majority could never impose their will upon the minority.

It was a defiant speech from the Great Nullifier, a last gesture from a dying man so concerned for property rights that he was ready to sacrifice the democratic principle of majority rule for them. Such an extreme proposal could win no popular support. It pleased only a handful of southern fire eaters. One by one the big guns of the Senate arose to speak on Clay's compromise. William H. Seward, the new Whig senator from New York, opposed it, appealing to a "higher law" to justify refusal of Constitutional protection to slavery. Jefferson Davis of Mississippi opposed it too, but on grounds similar to Calhoun's. The two Free Soilers in the Senate—Hale of New Hampshire and Chase of Ohio—opposed compromise. Democrats from both sections of the country—Cass of Michigan, Douglas of Illinois, Foote of Mississippi—supported Clay. The speech closest to the national mood, perhaps, was Daniel Webster's. The "godlike" Daniel, Whig senator from Massachusetts and eternally frustrated presidential hopeful, replied to Calhoun on March 7. It was the last great speech of a life spent in defense of the interests of tradition, property, and respectability. Webster supported Clay's plan in every respect. From the opening words of his speech—"I wish to speak today, not as a Massachusetts man, not as a northern man, but as an American"—he appealed to the belief of most Americans that their security, their liberty, their prosperity, was bound up with preservation of the Union. "I hold the idea of a separation of these States—those that are free to form one government, and those that are slaveholding to form another—as a moral impossibility."

He denounced the radical abolitionists and the radical secessionists as equal threats to the Union. There was no need for congressional action on slavery in the territories, he argued, because soil and climate would keep slavery out. He spoke at length on the fugitive slave issue, endorsing the South's demand for a harsher law:

Sir, here is a well-founded ground of complaint against the North, which ought to be removed, which it is now in the power of this government to remove; which calls for the enactment of proper laws authorizing the judicature of this government, in the several States, to do all that is necessary for the recapture of fugitive slaves and for their restoration to those who claim them. Wherever I go, and whenever I speak on the subject, and when I speak here I desire to speak to the whole North, I say that the South has been injured in this respect, and has a right to complain; and the North has been too careless of what I think the Constitution peremptorily and emphatically enjoins upon her as a duty.

His words were a stunning blow to many in his native New England. They had expected him to oppose Clay. "Benedict Arnold!" they cried out at him. "The man who has walked for years among the gods now has mingled with the apes," said Horace Mann. "The word *liberty* in the mouth of Webster sounds like the word *love* in the mouth of a courtesan," said Emerson.

In May, a Senate committee chaired by Clay reported

Daniel Webster.

the Kentuckian's compromise in the form of two bills. Webster's Seventh of March speech, it turned out, had enraged many Whigs in Congress and won few votes. But the opponents of Clay's compromise suffered a bad loss when, after a five-day illness, Zachary Taylor died in July. Acute indigestion, from eating too many cherries and drinking too much iced lemonade on a hot day, was said to be the cause. Ironically, no one regretted his going more than the Free Soilers who had so violently attacked him as a candidate. "Every day his position and policy were becoming more and more Northern," said the editor of the *National Era*. And as a slaveholder from a slave state Taylor had wielded more influence on the issue than a man from a free state could have. Taylor's death brought a champion of compromise to the White House, Millard Fillmore. The new President made Webster his Secretary of State, and teaming with Clay and Douglas they pushed through the compromise. By September 20, Clay's proposals, including the fugitive slave bill, were law.

A compromise? No, Clay admitted, more a southern victory than a compromise. But, he insisted, "there is, I believe, peace now prevailing throughout all our borders. I believe it is permanent." And President Fillmore too, hailed it as "a final settlement." It was what most citizens wanted to hear. They all prayed for peace.

But there were some who knew better. This "compromise," said Congressman Thaddeus Stevens, will become "the fruitful mother of future rebellion, disunion and civil war."

It did. Thirteen years after the Mexican War ended, the Civil War began.

Santy Anno

Guitar

Down

Ches - a - peake Bay ___ from Balt - i - more, A -

way, San - ty ___ An - no! ___

Round   Cape Horn   to   Fris - co __ Bay   All __

on   the   plains   of   Mex - i - co.

Chorus

Then heave   her up   and a - way we'll __ go, A -

way,   San - ty __ An - no! __

Heave her up and a - way __ we'll __ go, All __
on the plains of Mex - i - co.

Down Chesapeake Bay from Baltimore,
Away, Santy Anno!
Round Cape Horn to Frisco Bay
All on the Plains of Mexico.

CHORUS:
Then heave her up and away we'll go
Away, Santy Anno!
Heave her up and away we'll go,
All on the Plains of Mexico.

She's a fast clipper ship with a bully crew,
Away, Santy Anno!
A down-east Yankee for a captain too
All on the Plains of Mexico.

CHORUS

There's plenty of gold so I've been told
Away, Santy Anno!
There's plenty of gold so I've been told
All on the Plains of Mexico.

CHORUS

Back in the days of Forty-nine,
Away, Santy Anno!
Those were the days of the good old times,
All on the Plains of Mexico.

CHORUS

When Zack Taylor gained the day,
Away, Santy Anno!
He made poor Santy run away,
All on the Plains of Mexico.

CHORUS

Santy Anno was a good old man
Away, Santy Anno!
Till he went to war with Uncle Sam
All on the Plains of Mexico.

CHORUS

When I leave this ship I'll settle down
Away, Santy Anno!
Marry a girl named Sally Brown
All on the Plains of Mexico.

CHORUS

18

CONCLUSION

The war with Mexico rates many "firsts" in the record books. It was the first successful offensive war in American history. It was the first time American forces had occupied an enemy capital. It was the first time the United States had ruled under martial law on foreign soil. It was the first time the West Point Military Academy had contributed significant leadership to a war. It was the first time newspaper correspondents had reported a war from the battlefield. It was the first time that many leaders of the Civil War to come were schooled in combat—among them Grant, McClellan, Sherman, Hooker, Meade—who would wear the blue—and Lee, Jackson, Longstreet, Albert Sidney Johnston, Beauregard—who would wear the gray.

Another distinction of this war, and one less likely to be claimed for it in the textbooks, is that many people, like Ulysses S. Grant, thought it the most disgraceful war the country ever fought. They said this, to be sure, before the war in Vietnam. The historian Otis A. Singletary wrote recently that one reason why the Mexican War has been relatively neglected lies rooted in the guilt that we as a nation have come to feel about it. The undeniable fact that it was an offensive war so completely stripped it of moral pretensions that no politician of that era ever succeeded in elevating it to the lofty level of a "crusade." The additional fact that we paid Mexico fifteen million dollars after it was all over—"conscience money," as some called it—seemed to confirm the ugliest charges of those who denounced the war as a cynical land-grab from a neighbor too weak to defend herself.

Though it was a limited and not a total war, it was an event of profound influence upon our national life. Ralph Waldo Emerson foresaw its significance. "The United States will conquer Mexico," he wrote, "but it will be as the man who swallows the arsenic which brings him down in return. Mexico will poison us."

In the behavior of Congress and the Polk Administration during this war can be discerned a pattern that has marked the wars we have engaged in ever since. Frederick Merk, one historian who has most closely examined the way we got into the war with Mexico, has pointed this out:

A welling up of emotion, a rallying round the flag, a demand for quick revenge, is the response of men to news of an attack upon the homeland. When the attack is unprovoked (and the President had assured the nation this one was), when it is launched by Mexicans, and when it results in the shedding of American blood, frenzy is like to be the result. A government without ulterior purposes and genuinely loath to go to war asks Congress and the public to remain calm until the circumstances of the attack can be ascertained from the documents. A minority in Congress, if self-confident and courageous and given time, can hold up voting long enough to permit information to be gathered. The framers of the Constitution, in entrusting the war-making power to Congress, assumed that majorities would meet their responsibility and that alert minorities would have an even greater incentive to do so.

Such assumptions proved a house of cards in the voting of May 11–12 [1846]. An assault on an American force by a Mexican force had occurred, assuredly. But whether on American soil, and whether unprovoked—both highly controversial issues—were not inquired into, nor could they be in a day. An administration which had set the stage for the attack, would not be too much interested in an inquiry. It was content to have an uninformed vote, even a stampeded vote. It spurred on public opinion and Congress by the war message. As for the minority, it failed to perform its constitutional function.

How Polk conducted the war, once we were in it, also bears upon the Constitutional relationships between the President and the Congress. The historian Carl N. Degler holds that a political precedent of great and often damaging influence was set by Polk:

It was left to James Polk to explore the immense resources of power inherent in the President as Commander in Chief of the armed forces. Polk named the generals, set forth the grand strategy which won the war, cajoled and bullied the Congress into granting the necessary credits and support, and finally drew up the peace terms. All this was achieved with a minimum of consultation with or dependence upon the Congress. When faced with a much greater military challenge, Abraham Lincoln would find encouraging precedent in Polk's use of the Presidential power.

So would all the men who occupied the White House in the wars to come—the Spanish-American War, World War I, World War II, the Korean War, the war with Vietnam.

CHRONOLOGY

1845

March 1	President John Tyler signs joint resolution of Congress to annex Texas.
March 4	James K. Polk inaugurated President.
March 28	Mexico breaks off diplomatic relations with U.S.
July 31	General Zachary Taylor establishes base near Corpus Christi.
November 10	John Slidell dispatched to Mexico to restore peaceful relations.

1846

January 13	Taylor ordered to advance to Rio Grande.
March 12	Slidell mission fails.
March 28	Taylor reaches Rio Grande and begins building fort.
April 25	Mexican troops skirmish with U.S. forces. Polk begins to prepare war message for Congress.
May 8	Battle of Palo Alto.
May 9	Battle of Resaca de la Palma. Polk informs Cabinet that he believes he should send war message to Congress on May 12. Cabinet adjourns 2 P.M. News of April 25 skirmish reaches Polk 6 P.M. Second Cabinet meeting called at 7:30 P.M. Members agree that war message should be delivered May 11 rather than May 12.
May 11	Polk sends war message to Congress.
May 13	Congress declares existence of a state of war between Mexico and the U.S. by act of Mexico.

May 18	Taylor crosses the Rio Grande and occupies Matamoros.
June 3	Colonel Stephen Kearney ordered to occupy New Mexico and California.
June 14	"Bear Flag Revolt." Republic of California proclaimed by U.S. settlers.
June 16	Treaty between U.S. and Britain settles northern boundary of Oregon.
July 7	Commodore J. D. Sloat seizes Monterey and proclaims possession of California for U.S.
July 14	Taylor occupies Camargo.
August 8	Wilmot Proviso introduced in Congress, excluding slavery from any territory acquired from Mexico.
August 12	Commodore Stockton and Captain Frémont take Los Angeles.
August 16	Santa Anna returns to Mexico from exile.
August 18	Kearney occupies Santa Fe.
September 14	Santa Anna becomes commander-in-chief of Mexican army.
September 25	Taylor captures Monterrey, Mexico.
November 14	Commodore Conner takes Tampico.
November 16	Taylor takes Saltillo.
November 18	General Winfield Scott appointed commander of Gulf expedition in Mexico.
December 7	New session of Congress opens. Polk policy attacked, but war appropriations voted.

1847

January 3	Scott withdraws troops from Taylor.
February 22–23	Taylor defeats Santa Anna at Buena Vista.
March 8	U.S. landing at Vera Cruz.
March 29	Vera Cruz surrendered to Scott.
April 8	Scott begins advance on Mexico City.

April 15	Polk appoints Nicholas Trist commissioner to negotiate a peace with Mexico.
April 18	Scott defeats Mexicans at Cerro Gordo.
April 22	General Worth occupies Perote.
May 15	Worth occupies Puebla.
August 19	Battle of Churubusco.
August 24	Armistice agreed to at Tacubaya.
September 6	Armistice ended.
September 8	Battle of Molino del Rey.
September 13	Battle of Chapultepec.
September 14	Scott occupies Mexico City.
September 16	Santa Anna resigns Mexican presidency.
October 6	Polk orders Trist back to U.S.
November 16	Trist receives notice of recall.
December 4	Trist decides to stay in Mexico to negotiate.

1848

January 13	Polk relieves Scott of command.
January 24	Gold discovered in California.
February 2	Treaty of Guadalupe Hidalgo signed.
March 10	Treaty ratified by U.S. Senate.
March 25	Mexican government ratifies treaty.
June 12	U.S. forces leave Mexico City.
November 7	Zachary Taylor elected President.

BIBLIOGRAPHY

General

Important interpretations of the U.S. in the period of the war include Allan Nevins, *Ordeal of the Union* (2 volumes) (New York: Charles Scribner's Sons, 1947); Ray Allen Billington, *The Far Western Frontier 1830–1860* (New York: Harper & Row, 1956, paperback and hardcover); Roy F. Nichols, *The Stakes of Power 1845–1877*, (New York: Hill & Wang, 1961); and Chaplain W. Morrison, *Democratic Politics and Sectionalism: The Wilmot Proviso Controversy* (Chapel Hill: University of North Carolina Press, 1967).

The California & New Mexico Frontiers

In addition to Billington's *Far Western Frontier*, a superb account, there is Erna Fergusson's *New Mexico: A Pageant of Three Peoples* (New York: Alfred A. Knopf, Inc., 1951, 1964) and R. L. Duffus, *The Santa Fe Trail* (1930; paperback from University of New Mexico Press, 1972). Diaries and personal accounts include two used in this book, Richard Henry Dana, *Two Years Before the Mast* (1840; numerous paperback editions) and Josiah Gregg's *Commerce of the Prairies* (2 volumes) (1844; paperback from University of Nebraska Press, 1967). Also useful is *A Documentary History of the Mexican Americans*, edited by Wayne Moquin with Charles van Doren (New York: Praeger, 1971; Bantam Books, 1972).

Texas

The Texas question, inseparable from the Mexican War, is treated in many of the books listed here. Other accounts include Samuel H. Lowrie, *Culture Conflict in Texas 1821–1835* (1932; paperback from AMS Press, 1967); Eugene C. Barker, *Mexico and Texas 1821–1835* (1928; Russell Reprint, 1965) and John E. Weems, *Dream of Empire: A Human History of the Re-*

public of Texas 1836–1846 (New York: Simon & Schuster, 1971).

Manifest Destiny and the Causes of the War

A pioneering work, still one of the best, is Albert K. Weinberg, *Manifest Destiny* (1938: reissued as a Quadrangle paperback, 1963). Also of value is Frederick Merk, *Manifest Destiny and Mission in American History: A Reinterpretation* (New York: Alfred A. Knopf Inc., 1963). Debate on the causes of the war has given rise to a considerable literature. Contemporary abolitionists thought it was all the fault of the slaveholding South; see Theodore Parker, *The Slave Power* (1907; reissued as an Arno Press paperback, 1967); Wiliam Jay, *A Review of the Causes and Consequences of the Mexican War* (1849; reissued by Gregg, 1970); and John G. Palfrey, *Papers on the Slave Power* (Boston: Bobbs-Merrill, 1846).* A major historian, James Ford Rhodes, penned an indictment against the "aggressive slavocracy" in his *History of the United States from the Compromise of 1850,* vol. I (Chicago: University of Chicago Press, 1966, hardcover and paperback). On the other side, John D. P. Fuller, *The Movement for the Acquisition of All Mexico* (1936: reissued by Da Capo Press and Scholarly Books Inc. as paperbacks in 1969 and 1971 respectively), concludes Graebner, *Empire on the Pacific* (New York: Ronald Press, that slaveholders as a class were not behind the war. Norman 1955), holds that the drive of commercial interests for Pacific ports was a major cause of the expansionist movement against Mexico. Anthologies of scholarly writings which debate this issue of the causes of the conflict include Archie P. McDonald, *The Mexican War: Crisis for American Democracy* (Lexington: D. C. Heath, 1969), and Ramon Eduardo Ruiz, *The Mexican War: Was it Manifest Destiny?* (New York: Holt, Rinehart and Winston paperback, 1963). Popular dissent and political opposition to the war is fully covered in John H. Schroeder, *American Opposition and Dissent 1846–8* (Madison: University of Wis-

* Out of print.

consin Press, 1973). Works placing the blame for the war exclusively upon the Mexicans are included in the next section.

The Mexican War

Otis A. Singletary, *The Mexican War* (Chicago: University of Chicago Press, 1960, hardcover and paperback) provides a concise summary of the military campaigns. There are many memoirs and reports by participants, but, most remain out of print. See Robert Anderson, *An Artillery Officer in the Mexican War* (1911; reissued by Books for Libraries, 1972); William S. Henry, *Campaign Sketches of the War in Mexico* (1847: reissued by Arno Press, 1973); P. G. T. Beauregard, *With Beauregard in Mexico* (1956; reissued by Da Capo Press, 1969); and Ethan Allen Hitchcock, *Fifty Years in Camp and Field* (1909; reissued by Books for Libraries, 1972). For the California campaign, easily the best contemporary source is Erwin G. Gudde, ed., *Bigler's Chronicle of the West* (Berkeley: University of California Press, 1972). Selections from contemporary sources may be found in George Winston Smith and Charles Judah (eds.), *Chronicles of the Gringos: The U.S. Army in the Mexican War, 1846–1848* (Albuquerque: University of New Mexico Press, 1968); and Grady McWhiney and Sue McWhiney (eds.), *To Mexico with Taylor and Scott 1845–1847* (1969; paperback from Xerox College Publications, 1969).

The most detailed general history of the conflict is Justin H. Smith, *The War With Mexico* (1919; reissued by Peter Smith, 1963, 2 vols.). One-volume accounts which follow Smith in blaming the Mexicans and defending the U.S. role are Seymour V. Connor and Odie B. Faulk, *North America Divided: The Mexican War 1846–48* (New York: Oxford University Press, 1971), and Alfred Hoyt Bill, *Rehearsal for Conflict* (1947; reissued by Cooper Square, 1970).

The Mexican Side

For Spanish sources, see the bibliography in *North America Divided*, cited above. Works available in English include Justo Sierra, *The Political Evolution of the Mexican People* (Austin:

University of Texas Press, 1970); José Fernando Ramírez, *Mexico During the War with the United States* (St. Louis, Mo.: University of Missouri Press paperback, 1970, ed. Walter V. Scholes); and Ramon Alcarez, ed., *The Other Side: Or Notes for the History of the War between Mexico and the United States* (1850; reissued Burt Franklin, 1970).

Leading Figures

Autobiographies, biographies, letters and diaries are available for several of the most important political and military leaders. On President Polk there is Charles G. Sellers, *James K. Polk* (2 vols.) (Princeton: Princeton University Press, 1957–1966).* The *Diary of James K. Polk During his Presidency, 1845–1849* edited by Milo M. Quaife (4 vols.) (1910; Kraus Reprint, 1970) is of great value. For the general whose eary victories made him President, there is Holman Hamilton's *Zachary Taylor: Soldier of the Republic* (1941: reissued by The Shoe String Press, Archon Books, 1966). The life of the most prominent of the Mexican generals is found in Wilfred H. Callcott's *Santa Anna: The Story of an Enigma that Once Was Mexico* (1936; reprinted by Archon Books, The Shoe String Press, 1964).

Diplomacy

The best study of the diplomatic record is George L. Rives, *The United States and Mexico 1821–1848* (2 vols.) (1913: Kraus Reprint, 1969). Other accounts may be found in Jesse S. Reeves, *American Diplomacy Under Tyler and Polk* (Gloucester: Peter Smith, 1907) and James F. Rippy, *The United States and Mexico* (New York: Crofts, 1931, (rev. ed.)). Frederick Merk, *The Oregon Question: Essays in Anglo-American Diplomacy and Politics* (Cambridge: Harvard University Press, 1967) is a detailed and important study of British-American relations at the time of the war. The text of the treaty of Guadalupe Hidalgo may be found in many collections of historical documents.

* Volume 2 out of print.

ACKNOWLEDGMENTS

Grateful acknowledgment is made for permission to reprint copyrighted material:

Harvard University Press, *To Mexico With Scott: The Letters of Captain E. Kirby Smith to his Wife*, prepared by Emma J. Blackwood with an Introduction by R. M. Johnston, copyright © 1917. Reprinted by permission of Harvard University Press; Louisiana State University Press, *With Beauregard in Mexico: The Mexican War Reminiscences of P. G. T. Beauregard*, edited by T. Harry Williams, copyright © 1956 by Louisiana State University Press; Princeton University Press, *James K. Polk, Volume II, Continentalist 1843–1846* by Charles G. Sellers. Copyright © 1966 by Princeton University Press. Reprinted by permission of Princeton University Press; G. P. Putnam's Sons, *Fifty Years in Camp and Field* by Ethan Allen Hitchcock, copyright © 1909; and *An Artillery Officer in the Mexican War* by Robert Anderson, copyright © 1911. Reprinted by permission of G. P. Putnam's Sons; The University of Missouri Press, *Mexico During the War with the United States* by José Fernando Ramírez, edited by Walter V. Scholes, translated by Elliot B. Scherr. Copyright © 1970 by the Curators of the University of Missouri. Reprinted by permission of the University of Missouri Press; The University of Texas Press, *The Political Evolution of the Mexican People* by Justo Sierra, translated by C. Ramsdell, copyright © 1970. Reprinted by permission of The University of Texas Press.

Grateful acknowledgment is made for the use of illustrations:

American Antiquarian Society, 117; Bancroft Library, University of California, Berkeley, 109; The Bettmann Archive, 81; Anne S. K. Brown Military Collection, Brown University Library, 163; Chicago Historical Society, 219; Gilcrease Collection, 96; Granger Collection, 60, 91, 122, 147; Library of Congress, 20, 31, 101, 151, 223, 232, 250; Metropolitan Museum of Art, 255; New-York Historical Society, 23, 63, 73, 212, 227, 241; New York Public Library Picture Collection, 77, 141, 192, 215; Peabody Museum, Harvard University, 15; Henry T. Peters, Jr., 48; Polk Home, 51, 67; Rodolfo Pulido G., 175, 177, 179; Franklin D. Roosevelt Library, 133; San Jacinto Museum of History Association, 129, 204; The Smithsonian Institution, 159; Texas State Library, 39; West Point Museum Collections, *jacket*, 113; Yale University Library, 153.

INDEX

Milton Meltzer, historian and biographer, is the author of more than twenty-five books. His previous books for *The Living History Library* are *Brother, Can You Spare a Dime? The Great Depression 1929–1933* and *Bread—and Roses: The Struggle of American Labor 1865–1915*. One of his recent works, *Hunted Like a Wolf*, deals with the Seminole War, in which slavery was a major issue, as in the Mexican War that followed. Among his other works are the two-volume world history *Slavery; The Right to Remain Silent; Underground Man*, a novel about the abolitionists; *Remember the Days: A Short History of the Jewish American*; and *In the Eye of Conscience: Photography and Social Change*.

Born in Worcester, Massachusetts, Mr. Meltzer was educated at Columbia University. He and his wife live in New York City. They have two daughters.

John Anthony Scott has taught at Columbia and Amherst colleges and from 1951 to 1968 was Chairman of the Department of History at the Fieldston School, New York, where he still teaches. He is also a Professor of Legal History at Rutgers University. Among the numerous books he has authored or edited are *The Ballad of America, Trumpet of a Prophecy*, and *Teaching for a Change*.

973.6 Meltzer, Milton
ME

Bound for the Rio
Grande: the Mexican
struggle, 1845-1850

DATE			